# SPIRITS OF THE NIGHT

## THE *VAUDUN* GODS OF HAITI

### SELDEN RODMAN

and

### CAROLE CLEAVER

Foreword by Jay Livernois

Spring Publications, Inc.
Dallas, Texas

94-112

The paintings are not of the *loas*, but for the *loas*.

SPRING PUBLICATIONS, INC.; P.O. BOX 222069; DALLAS, TX 75222

Cover and interior art designed and produced by Julia Hillman. The cover image
is from the painting, *Spirits of the Night,* by the Haitian artist Ramphis Magloire.
Photographed by Jonathan Lam from the
collection of Mark Seidenfeld, New York City, New York.

ISBN 0-88214-354-9

# CONTENTS

# ACKNOWLEDGMENTS

Carla Rodman, the artist who drew the *vevers* reproduced at the beginning of the chapters, attended her first *vaudun* ceremony before she was born (she liked the beat) and viewed many thereafter.

Special thanks go to the following people for their kind permission to reproduce works from their Haitian art collections: Charles Boer, Don Garrabrant, Julia Hillman, Jay Livernois, Mark Seidenfeld, and Mr. and Mrs. Maurice C. Thompson.

And a special thanks goes to the Haitian artists and people; may their country one day know the peace, freedom and prosperity it deserves.

# Illustrations

Overleaf:

Selden Rodman and Lafortune Félix
Photo by Bill Negron

Carole Cleaver and Ramphis Magloire
Photo by Selden Rodman

Overleaf:

**Erzulie**
by Hector Hyppolite, 1947.
Private Collection

**Erzulie**
by Gérard, 1989.
Collection, Jay Livernois, Woodstock, Connecticut

# FOREWORD

## *DEEP IN THE HEART OF HAITI*

"Any bullets?" were the first words said to me in Haiti. It was 7 January 1985, in the Dr. François Duvalier Airport, Port-au-Prince. I was going through Customs. I expected something like this, but not quite.

The Duvaliers were still in power. "Baby Doc" ruled, but not with the overt paranoia and sadism of his father, "Papa Doc," who had died in 1973. The Duvaliers' political security militia, the *Tonton Macoutes,* were around but were supposedly semi-retired, or so it seemed to a *blanc* (a white) on winter vacation from New England. I was more interested in the obvious Caribbean sun's warmth than the subtle political heat that was about to explode a little more than a year later.

The big news out of Haiti and coming to America at that time was not political but medical. Haiti was being blamed as the country of origin of AIDS, and Haitians were foolishly black-listed as the international carriers of the disease. Some Americans even believed AIDS was perhaps in the water and air of Haiti, and that just sunning on the beach would be enough to catch it. As a result of these rumors, I seemed to be one of only two non-Haitians on the jet from New York City to Port-au-Prince.

Haiti was and is the poorest nation in the Western Hemisphere. Besides AIDS Haiti was and is rife with diseases from malaria to tuberculosis to leprosy to yaws. Haiti had never had a free election, and its governments were routinely corrupt if not brutal dictatorships.

I "knew" that the people of Haiti were dominated by "voodoo," which at that time I assumed to be a collection of left-over African superstitions with no connection to any of the major religious traditions. I also thought that its power was only effective with gullible, poor, "black" people and easily faded in the light of reason and a better standard of living. Still I was warned in a whisper not to leave hair or fingernail clippings around my hotel sink. And every outsider going to Haiti was aware that a "zombie" was not just a name of a rum and fruit juice drink at a bar. In going to Haiti for a vacation, there was a vague Hollywood fear that with one wrong turn, one wrong word, or a glance at the wrong person, and you could end up the next day with a rag doll on your bed looking like you, filled with pins. Then the fun would begin.

I "knew" all this and was prepared not to be surprised when I saw a country and people living under these conditions. A part of me wanted to go into this Heart of Darkness, but of course only with my cultural eyes and heart closed, and with my politically correct radar on. So the question, "Any bullets?" did not surprise me; it thrilled me as I stammered out a "—Nnno" in reply.

But there were other, more vague reasons of why I had come to Haiti. I had heard that an interesting kind of art had developed there, although it was termed "primitive" by the Modernist art critics and historians I read. It was mentioned particularly in reference to the French Surrealists who had "discovered" it in the 1940's. I figured this art at least was exotic, and exotic in the best sense of that term. Bored with the late Modernist art preoccupations of my world in 1985, I wanted to see Haitian art and its place of origin firsthand, and the exotic.

The person most often referred to in connection with this Haitian "primitive" art was an American man of letters, Selden Rodman (he was even mentioned in the guide-books). I knew that he was not only a well-known expert on Haitian art but of "primitive" art of the Americas as well, and that he was a literary critic, poet, and anthologist. The blues and jazz producer-historian, Sam Charters, had told me that Rodman's anthology, *100 Modern Poets,* was one of the best collections of poetry he had ever read. The heretical classicist Charles Boer had also said that he had heard about Rodman through his friend, the poet Charles Olson. Olson had known him in the 1940's when Rodman was the poetry editor of *Portfolio* magazine (published by Caresse Crosby of Black Sun Press fame) in Washington, D.C.

I found out that Selden Rodman lived a good part of the year in Haiti in the southern coastal coffee port town of Jacmel. There he had a house and an art gallery called *Renaissance II.* A travel book on Haiti said that there was in Jacmel a small, pleasant, two story hotel, called the Jacmeli-enne, run by a woman from New York. It was described as sitting on a black sand beach, with a pool, a bar, a good res-taurant, and tennis.

I was able to pay for my trip with the money from a job writing a biographical piece on Kate Douglas Wiggin, the Victorian American author most famous for her children's novel, *Rebecca of Sunnybrook Farm.* I seemed to sense that, given my head, the combination of a Victorian children's lit-erature author and Haiti would make an interesting mix.

So I went through Customs at the Dr. François Duvalier Airport, and after a rather round-about trip on an exotically painted, semi-public bus (called a *Tap-Tap*) over the moun-tains to the southern coast of Haiti, I got to the hotel. Al-though it was late, dinner was still being served. The meal consisted of a fine main dish of goat and vegetables, and the wine was good and inexpensive (unusual for the Caribbean). A four-piece local band played in the dim atmosphere of the restaurant foyer, and as in the movies, drums could be heard in the distance. And so to bed.

The next day I asked the "New Yorkaise" owner of the hotel, Marlene Danies, where the tennis courts were. They didn't seem to be on the grounds of the hotel, and I hadn't seen any the night before while driving through Jacmel to get to the hotel. It was difficult to see as the town was lit by a strange combination of small charcoal cooking fires and electrical street lights which would go on and off depending on the power surges coming from the local electrical generating plant.

She told me, "Unfortunately the hotel doesn't have any, but there is a tennis court down the street. You have to speak with Mr. Rodman to arrange to play. He has the key to the court."

I asked, "How do I speak to Mr. Rodman to use the court?"

She said, "He opens his gallery in the afternoon, and he'll be glad to talk to you about tennis then." So it seemed I was to meet Selden Rodman sooner than I would have thought, and I was to do it through tennis.

That afternoon I made my way to Rodman's gallery and home up the street from the Jacmelienne. It was a beautiful, three story, nineteenth century French Caribbean style townhouse, painted in bright blue and white. A sign with a mermaid (the Haitian goddess *La Sirène*) hung out in front announcing, **SELDEN RODMAN**—*Renaissance II*.

The heavy metal ground level doors were open but no one seemed to be around. I gave a "hallo," and an assistant appeared from out of somewhere. He directed me up the stairs, and as I was going up, Selden was coming down.

I don't remember what was said this first time we met (my memory of it is a white darkness), but I was hit by Selden's appearance and soft-spokenness which projected a sense of utter calm. He was dressed in a white embroidered Caribbean shirt, white pants, and wore oversized sun-glasses. He graciously gave me a tour of the gallery and his house. In the middle of the dining room, a large table was filled with books, papers and a typewriter. He was working on a book about Mozart's letters. Mozart's *Jupiter Symphony* could be heard quietly playing on a stereo in the background..

What impressed me then and still impresses me now was the unusual elegance of not just the man but the unique combination that he put together of Haitian culture, Mozart, literary creation, and personality. I had long been interested in James Hillman's ideas on psychology, polytheism, and Renaissance culture, and here before me was a man who was living it. And living it, because deep in the heart of Haiti (with its *vaudun* religion), there is a living polytheistic culture. Its collective soul and place is multifaceted, colored, and not given to the blank monotheistic obsessions which leads us always to try to "recover." Instead Haiti is tolerant and indulgent of the gods and their pleasures. When European culture sees Haiti, only its pathology, economic poverty, and dark side is seen. Hence the popular image of *vaudun* in Haiti as a cult of blood sacrifices, madness, greed, and cannibalism, and not of gentleness, healing, and imagination.

After the initial meeting with Selden, we arranged to play tennis later that evening. With tennis we became friends, and I have gotten to know his wife, Carole, as well. What always impresses me about them, and adds to their charm as people, is their complete and total lack of racism. This is held by them so effortlessly, it easily complements their exceptional openness to people and the world. They live multi-culturalism without any agenda or arrogance. They just do it as they have done it for years.

For the rest of my stay in Jacmel, I visited Selden and Carole every day. I got to know their hospitality, backgammon games with their son Van, their wonderful Haitian rum punches, their literary conversations. But, again and again, each time I visited them, my imagination was simply blown apart by their collection of Haitian art. *That* was a religious experience. And that is *vaudun!*

——Jay Livernois

## *Ogoun*, God of War

The embodiment of the male principle, signifying strength and power, *Ogoun's* symbol is a sword and his color is red. Descended from the Nigerian god of lightning, *Ogoun* is associated with fire and metal, and *Ogoun Feraille* is the patron of blacksmiths. Identified with St. Jacques, he is often shown in military uniform, riding a white horse and waving the national flag. His appearance is sometimes greeted with the playing of the national anthem. *Ogoun* drinks rum and prefers the sacrifice of a red cock.

# CHAPTER ONE

## WHAT YOU READ IS NOT NECESSARILY THE TRUTH

Who wants to read about the gentleness and humor of the typical Haitian? Who wants to believe that *vaudun* (popularly rendered as "voodoo"), the African-Caribbean spirit cult of the peasants, is a religion of psychic healing, generally benevolent, never fanatical and warlike as Christianity and Islam have so often been, not bloodthirsty, but fulfilling the daily needs of its worshippers and providing its major artists with the kind of deeply rooted folklore and metaphysics all great arts build upon?

Does anyone care to hear this from the mouths of a succession of poets and scholars? To read the scrupulous anthropologists like Jean Price-Mars and Harold Courlander? Or the renowned scholars like James G. Leyburn and Robert Farris Thompson at Yale? Or the poet-savants of international fame like André Breton and André Malraux of France, whose testimonies are common currency? It is so much easier to read a young sensationalist like Wade Davis, who would have you believe that zombies in hordes are being raised from the dead all over Haiti, or to see the disreputable movie based on his book. In our more than fifty years traveling and living in every part of Haiti, we have never encountered a *zombie* or found a reputable Haitian who generalizes from isolated instances of quacks administering soporific drugs to the dying.

Certainly central to American misconceptions is the *vaudun* religion, which conjures up images of spells, curses, witchcraft, and dolls attacked by pins. "Voodoo" is now commonly used as a synonym for "magic," which *vaudun* clearly is not.[1] The serenity and beauty of Haiti—its common people, their African-Caribbean religion, and the arts that celebrate it—are in stark contrast to the image of Haiti projected in the rest of the world.

For example Haiti was planning to hold its first free and fair election in more than thirty years. The hopes of millions of suffering, desperate people were pinned on this event. At a New York city dinner party a grinning intellectual said to us, "The real question is, 'Should the zombies vote?'"

We didn't laugh. We didn't think it was funny. For decades Haiti has been so maligned, so joked about, so misunderstood that we few Americans who know and love that country have lost our sense of humor.

Articles in magazines like *Playboy* and *Vanity Fair*, movies like *I Walked With A Zombie*, depict only terror and perversion; books like Wade Davis' *The Serpent and the Rainbow*, Elisabeth Abbott's *Haiti: The Duvaliers and Their Legacy*, Amy Wilentz's *The Rainy Season,* permit themselves no reference at all to the peasants' religion as practiced in the countryside, or to the transcendental arts whose subject is an unflagging *joie de vivre*. Like most Latin-American countries and all underdeveloped ones, Haiti has never enjoyed democracy as we have in the United States. Its people have always

---

[1]Ever since George Bush's campaign for the Republican presidential nomination in 1980 coined the phrase "voodoo economics" to criticize Ronald Reagan's proposed economic "reforms," the word "voodoo" has appeared in very strange places. Even so august a publication as the *New York Times* reviewed a satire as "voodoo theater" because its object was to "stick verbal pins into effigies of theatrical enemies."

been at the mercy of domestic corruptionists or foreign imperialists ready to take advantage of their vulnerability. So those intellectuals who come to Haiti seeking only corroboration for self-serving apocalyptic conclusions, find what they are looking for, *and nothing else.* Since there are no reliable sources, no free press, the most bizarre stories, always unverified, are printed as *facts.*

Demonology, as expressed in ceremonies devoted to the *Guédés* (spirits or *loas* of death) and *Baron Samedi* of the cemeteries, has always fascinated such artist-*houngans* (priests of *vaudun*) as Hector Hyppolite, André Pierre, Lafortune Félix, Edger Jean-Baptiste, and occasionally such visionary mystics as Pauléus Vital and Gérard Paul. More recently the two talented sons of Louisiane St. Fleurant, Stivenson and Ramphis Magloire, have resorted to this imagery in some of their paintings to express (though they might deny it) their unease over such recent tragic events as General Henri Namphy's shoot-out of the November 1987 elections; the massacre of Père Aristide's congregation at church which led to the tyrant Namphy's expulsion from Haiti a year later; and the political and economic uncertainty that hangs over Haiti in the wake of President Aristide's expulsion by the military.

Yet this imagery comes from *vaudun* which is the religion of the Haitian people. Through almost five centuries of trial and error (since African slaves were brought to the Caribbean to work alongside and eventually replace Amerindians enslaved by the Spanish) devotees of *vaudun* have developed rituals to please and even *materialize* their gods. A *vaudun* ceremony, like a Christian service, consists of prayers, chants, and offerings. But while Christian offerings are almost always monetary, *vaudun* offerings are far more personal. "The difference between the Haitian gods and the white man's gods," a *houngan* told us, "is that Haitian *loas* must eat." Like humans who become weak if they are not properly fed, Haitian gods, when not fed, lose their power. The actions between the people and their gods are reciprocal. If the devotee supports the god with sustenance to keep it strong, in troubled times the god will use that strength to support the devotee in return. Thus Haitian gods are offered fruits, grains, doves, chickens, rum, sweet colas, goats, bulls and pigs. Since money is always in short supply, it has been easier for the people of Haiti to offer these things. Indeed it is often by the produce of their land and the size of their flocks that the wealth of rural people is counted. It is no stranger for a peasant to kill a chicken to feed his gods than it is for him to kill one to feed his family. Those of us who have been sheltered by the bloodless and sanitized mechanics of supermarkets may be horrified by the idea of "blood sacrifice," but for country people the killing of animals for food is an everyday, normal act. Some *loas*, it is true, are content to be "vegetarians," satisfied by corn meal and sweets, but others require a sturdier diet.

There are hundreds, perhaps thousands of *vaudun* spirits, each with a special taste of its own. The original spirits were *les morts*, the spirits of the dead. Just as a child sought aid from its parents, an adult might ask help from an ancestor who had passed into the world beyond. Some of the dead were stronger than others, able to give better council and effect better cures. When a family *loa* was seen to be especially wise and helpful, it soon began to receive offerings from others and was elevated to the level of a local god or *mystère*. A pantheon of gods developed, each with its own characteristics and tastes. Every *loa* was identified with a specific color and demanded to be "served" specific foods when summoned by the drawing of its design, or *vever*, and the sound of specific chants and rhythms at its *cérémonie*.

Few visitors to Haiti have not been awakened in the night by the sound of drums. On the dark, distant mountains, in the villages of the valleys, the drums call—call *serviteurs* to chant, dance, worship together—call the Haitian gods to come forth with healing, benevolence and blessings.

If the *cérémonie* is successful a true communion will take place. The spirits will enter, possess, and speak through the mouths of the faithful. For a few magic moments, Love and War, Sea and Wood, Eros and Death, will take human form and live.

Each Haitian will have transcended his earthly poverty, desperation, and pain to enter the cosmos and become one with a god. Through centuries of slavery, deprivation, and fear, the ecstasy of that experience, the intuitive knowledge of a world beyond, has enabled Haitians not merely to endure, but to know joy

Haitian art exemplifies this joy. Its perennial subjects are the joys of life and afterlife, often expressing this through images of *vaudun*. Why is this so?

A partial answer was first brought home to us during the winter of 1973 on the verandah of the Grand Hotel Oloffson in Port-au-Prince. We had been helping Richard and Erna Flagg buy Haitian art for a collection that was later to be donated to the Milwaukee Art Museum. An American tourist came up to our table and asked Flagg how he could be happy in a country where so many people were so miserable. "Miserable!" he exclaimed. "I find people in the richest country in the world truly miserable, unhappy to find no satisfaction at all in the material things money can buy; hating themselves and even their country; aimless and bored. Here in Haiti, by contrast, I find even the poorest citizen happy with the little he has, capable of laughing at the foibles of the rich and at himself, filled with *joie de vivre* as we in the West no longer are. And all of this is reflected triumphantly in their art."

Why are the Haitian people almost alone in the world today feeling this rapport with things as they are? and in reflecting so much joy from it in their art? This climate existed briefly in rural Yugoslavia three or four decades ago, and in remote parts of Brazil, Mexico and even, more recently, in the South and West of the United States. But nowhere has a whole school of art, the dominant, self-taught art of a nation, embodied such values—and done so consistently over a period of more than forty years—as in Haiti.

The reasons for this are deep-rooted and complex, and one must go back in Haitian history from 1804 to 1944, to come up with complete answers. Certainly one factor in Haiti's former pattern of peace and contentment (with very little in the way of what the West considers "the good things of life" to show for it) was solidified during the second half of the nineteenth century. Under a succession of venal emperors and unprincipled dictators, black as well as mulatto, with one caste violently succeeding its predecessor only to repeat the same pilfering of public funds, the overwhelming majority of Haitians—the peasants—shunned politics. These peasants, meanwhile, were achieving their spiritual satisfaction from *vaudun*, entrenched in the countryside and pervasive during the century Haiti had been virtually sealed off from the rest of the world.

Many attempts to stamp out the peasants' religion have been made, most recently by the brutal General Namphy, aided and abetted by some of the rival Christian groups, but so far all have failed. If *vaudun* does vanish, the arts of Haiti will vanish with it. And so may the pride and independent spirit of the Haitian people who without it are likely to fall back on an alien god—or no god at all—in a frantic effort to "keep up" with the outside world's surrender to material comforts and values.

---

Facing page:

**Agoué and His Consort**
by Hector Hyppolite, 1947.
Mr. and Mrs. Maurice C. Thompson, Wilton, Connecticut

# *Erzulie,* Goddess of Love

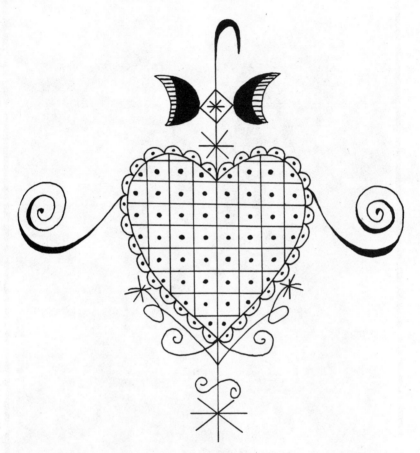

*Erzulie*, also known as *Erzulie Fréda Dahomey* is the *Rada* goddess of romance and dreams. The essence of the female principle, she delights in perfume, make-up, jewelry, sweet cakes and champagne. Her colors are pink and blue, her symbol a checkered heart, and her chosen sacrifice, a white dove. Although she wears three wedding rings for her three husbands—*Ogoun, Damballah,* and *Agoué*—she is identified with the Virgin Mary. She loves to give and receive gifts and is worshipped by those in search of luxury. After donning beautiful clothes, dancing, and playing the coquette, those who are possessed by *Erzulie* soon begin to weep for their lost loves and unfulfilled dreams.

# CHAPTER TWO

## WHAT IS *VAUDUN* (VOODOO)

Voodoo in Haiti is a profound and vitally alive religion—alive as Christianity was in its beginnings and in the early Middle Ages when miracles and mystical illuminations were common everyday occurrances...The high gods enter by the back door and abide in the servants' lodge...It has been a habit of all gods from immemorial days. They have shown themselves singularly indifferent to polite company, high-sounding titles, parlors and fine houses...indifferent indeed to all worldly pride and splendor. We have built domed temples and vast cathedrals, baited with glories of polychrome and marble to trap them, but when the gods come uninvited of their own volition, or send their messengers, or drop their flamescript cards of visit from the skies, it is not often these gilded temples or the proud of the earth they seek, but rather some road-weary humble family asleep in a wayside stable, some illiterate peasant dreaming in an orchard as she tends her sheep, some cobbler in his hut among the Alps.

--William Seabrook[1]

*Vaudun* is a living religion, and where still practiced devoutly is as integrated a governor of man's whole life as any religion in the world today. Those, as James Leyburn ob-

---

[1]William Seabrook, *The Magic Island*, (New York: Paragon House, 1929, rpt. 1989), pp. 12-13.

serves,[2] who conceive of religion in terms of orthodoxy, monotheism, sin, moral law, eternal rewards and punishments, will not understand *vaudun* at all, because, for one thing, its conception of spirits is anthropomorphic. No one is wholly good or wholly evil nor is any god. Failing to recognize the Occidental dualism between spirit and matter, and therefore placing no premium on asceticism, the *vaudunist* regards the sensual body and the aspiring soul as one; and like the Oriental, as the celebrated filmmaker, the late Maya Deren pointed out,[3] he predicates his faith "on the notion that truth can be apprehended only when every cell of brain and body—the totality of a human being—is engaged in that pursuit." Far from making a primary virtue, as we do, of self-restraint, the *vaudunist's* whole drive is toward participation in the *vaudun* religion, and therefore the person who becomes "possessed" (or, as they say, "mounted" by the *loa* that then speaks through his temporarily unhoused body) has achieved the final aim of his faith: communication with the gods.

Like Deren, Dr. Stanley Reser, an American psychiatrist of Scandinavian descent, whom we knew in the 1940's when he was superintendent of the hospital for the insane at Point Beudet, was one of the few foreigners to have been accepted as a *vaudun* devotee himself. "Doc", as the Haitians called him, preferred to define *vaudun* in terms of the *vaudunist's* well-known ability to handle live coals or to effect surprising medical cures. "Nothing in this world," he liked to say, "is supernatural, but many things are inexplicable or 'abnormal.' The Haitian peasant is simply closer to nature, and has been for hundreds of years, than we are; so empirically he is in

---

[2]James G. Leyburn, *The Haitian People*, (New Haven: Yale University Press, 1941), p. 143.
[3]Maya Deren, *Divine Horsemen: The Living Gods of Haiti*, (New York: Thames & Hudson, 1953), p. 9.

close touch with the laws of nature, many of which are still beyond our comprehension."[4]

Since one never sees the same *vaudun* ceremony twice, since practices vary from place to place and from time to time, and since "authorities" seldom agree on the meaning of any ceremonial object or specific symbol, the difficulties involved in attempting to describe the rites succinctly are manifest. Not every aspect will be of equal interest to the average reader. Nor would a description of any one, or two, or three *cérémonies* be likely to coincide with any one, two, or three that one is likely to witness. This being said, we would like to move on to the origins of *vaudun*.

*Voodoo* or *vodun* or *vaudun*, although traced by some scholars to a corruption of the French word *Vaudois* (meaning a Waldensian or heretic), is probably synonymous with the identical West African word for spirit. *Vaudou* is first mentioned by Moreau de St.-Méry, a French intellectual who had spent ten years in the French colony of St. Domingue (which became Haiti) just before the slave insurrection of 1791. If one discounts the patronizing tone taken by all Europeans of the period to anything colonial or non-European, his description of *vaudun* is acute as well as prophetic.

> It is very natural to think that Voodoo owes its origin to the serpent cult, to which the people of Juida are particularly devoted. They also say that it originated in the kingdom of Ardra, which, like Juida, is on the Slave Coast. And how far the Africans push their superstitions in regard to this animal, the adder, is easy to recognize from what I have just told.
>
> What is very true of Voodoo and at the same time very remarkable, is the spirit of hypnotism, which brings the members to dance right to the edge of consciousness. The prevention of spying (it may be added) is very rigorous. Whites caught ferreting out the secrets of the sect and tapped by a member who has

---

[4]Marcus Bach, *Strange Altars,* (New York: Bobbs Merrill, 1952). *Strange Altars* by Marcus Bach is based on his introduction to Haitian *vaudun* with Dr. Reser as his mentor.

spotted them have sometimes themselves started dancing and have consented to pay the Voodoo Queen to put an end to this punishment. I cannot fail to add, however, that never has any man of the constabulary, who has sworn war upon Voodoo, not felt the power which compels him to dance and which without doubt has saved the dancers from any need for flight.

In order to quiet the alarms which this mysterious cult of Voodoo causes in the Colony, they affect to dance it in public, to the sound of the drums and of rhythmic hand clapping. They even have this followed by a dinner where people eat nothing but poultry. But I assure you that this is only one more calculation, to evade the watchfulness of the magistrates and the better to guarantee the success of this dark cabal. After all, Voodoo is not a matter of amusement or enjoyment. It is rather a school where those easily influenced give themselves up to a domination which a thousand circumstances can render tragic.

One would not credit to what extent the Voodoo chiefs keep other members in dependence on them. There is no one of these latter who would not prefer anything to the evils with which they are threatened if they don't go regularly to the assemblies or don't blindly do what they are ordered to do. One can see that fright has influenced them, to make them abandon the use of reason. In a word, nothing is more dangerous, according to all the accounts, than this cult of Voodoo. It can be made into a terrible weapon—this extravagant idea that the ministers of this alleged god know all and can do anything.[5]

Early *vaudun* was indeed based on the serpent cult of Dahomey,[6] and snakes, though no longer introduced into ritual, continue to play a symbolic and decorative role. It was Boukman, a *papaloi* or priest (the word *houngan* is now used) who employed *vaudun* in its most aggressive form (*Pétro*) to summon the slaves to revolt in 1791. Boukman was killed. But the later leaders of the successful slave revolt, Toussaint Louverture, Jean-Jacques Dessalines and Henry Christophe,

---

[5] Moreau de St. Méry, *A Civilization that Perished*, trans. Ivor Spencer, (Lanham, MD: University Press of America, 1985), pp. 5-7.
[6] Robert Farris Thompson, *Flash of the Spirit*, (New York: Random House, 1983), p. 164.

prohibited *vaudun* entirely, Dessalines with the bayonet; it prevented regimentation for work and posed too great a challenge to absolute power. The first mulatto president, Alexandre Pétion, tolerated *vaudun* as he tolerated most things; and during the seventy years of the Catholic exclusion that followed, the beliefs of *vaudun* assumed their present characteristic shape.

The *cérémonies* are a series of graphic demonstrations of the forces of nature symbolized by the various *loas* and of the participant's capacity to integrate with them. Every ceremony begins with a salutation to the *mystères*, following which the *houngan* lights a candle and draws a *vever* (by dribbling flour or ashes through the fingers) appropriate to the *loa* or *loas* being summoned.[7] It is supposed the *vevers*, since they are foreign to African rites and somewhat resemble North Amerindian sand drawings, were introduced into *vaudun* by survivors of the aboriginal people of Haiti.[8] Intricate and very beautiful when skillfully drawn, the *vevers* serve no purpose once they are completed and are therefore danced on until they vanish. *Hounsis*, the priest's female attendants and dancing chorus, now enter, dressed in white, and perform gestures and prayers designed to adjust the relationships of the various participants. The prayer, sometimes in *Créole* and

---

[7] "The *serviteur* learns love and beauty in the presence of *Erzulie*, experiences the ways of power in the diverse aspects of *Ogoun*, becomes familiar with the aspects of death in the attitudes of *Guédé*. He sings in the chorus, and feels in his own person that surge of security which is harmonious with collective action. He witnesses the wisdom of ancestral and divine counsel, and learns the advantages of accepting such counsel, with its history and experience, for his own guidance in action. In effect, he understands the principles because he sees them function." Deren, *op. cit.*, p. 194.

[8] The presence of Masonic elements, like the eye and the compass, points to another origin of *vevers* perhaps in pre-Revolutionary French Colonial secret societies. It also seems that maybe the jigsaw work and the elaborate iron gates embellished with curlicues imported from France contributed to the lace-like tracery of the *vevers*.

sometimes in *langage* (a vestigial African tongue understood only by the *loas* themselves), may last for hours. The sacrifice, the climax of the ceremony, which follows, depends for its character on circumstances.

A *mangé loa*, at which the deity is sustained with food and drink, is the ceremony most frequently performed, and may take place anywhere, lasting a matter of hours or days. Baptismal *cérémonies* are closely related to the *mangé loa*. But the next stage of a *serviteur's* progress, in terms of the hierarchy within the *houmfor*, is the series of rites known as *canzo* or initiation; once graduated, a *canzo* initiate is thereafter a full-fledged participant in all *cérémonies*, outranked only by the *houngan* and his immediate assistants. *Canzo cérémonies*, and their ultimate stage, the *brulé-zin* or trial by fire, are akin to death-and-resurrection in their symbolism: the initiate is covered with a sheet during his ordeal which involves handling hot meal or walking over live coals.

As a further explanation of the *cérémonies* and their functioning in relation to *loas*, it is probably the time to explain that *vaudun*, like other polytheistic religions, has a pantheon of gods, both major and minor. In the *Rada* branch of *vaudun*, the principal *loas* are *Damballah* and *Aida-Wedo; Erzulie; Legba; Agoué* and *Maîtresse La Sirène; Guédé* (*Baron Samedi* is one of *Guédé's* manifestations); *Loco* and *Aïzan; Papa 'Zaca*; and *Ogoun Feraille*.

*Damballa Wedo*, the ancient Dahomean rain god, and his wife *Aida-Wedo*, are imagined respectively as a heavy boa constrictor and a narrow green snake. *Aida-Wedo* is also seen in the form of the rainbow. Chickens are sacrificed to both gods, both control fertility, and in Haiti both are associated with white. *Damballah* is sometimes identified with the Roman Catholic St. Patrick who is also connected to serpents in legend and symbol.

*Erzulie Fréda Dahomey*, goddess of the home, of purity and of love, is invoked by a checkered heart symbol and is identified in Haiti with the Christian Virgin Mary. She is not to be confused with *Erzulie Ze rouge* (red eyes), an erotic, evil goddess from another branch of *vaudun*, *Pétro*.

---

Overleaf:

***Damballah*** **Helmeted**
by Hector Hyppolite,1947.
Collection, Musée d'Art Haïtian, Port-au-Prince, Haiti

**The *Loa Damballah***
by Prospère Pierrelouis, 1987.
Collection, Jay Livernois, Woodstock, Connecticut

*Legba,* well-known in Africa as a seducer of women and a mischief-maker, is known in Haiti as a kindly old man, but he still has to do with fertility and likes sacrifices of goats and roosters. *Legba cérémonies* begin with a song to him and the sprinkling of a few drops of rum on the ground in his honor. *Legba's* Roman Catholic equivalent is St. Peter. He opens the way from the material to the spiritual world (as a syncretic image the keys of St. Peter tie in nicely with *Legba*). And like the Greek Hermes, *Legba* is a liminal god.

*Agoué* and his spouse *La Sirène* are gods of the sea and the islands therein. *Agoué* is symbolized by a boat-drawing and sacrifices to him are often loaded on small barques and set adrift at sea. His wife takes the shape of a mermaid. Fishermen are naturally much concerned with propitiating these *loas.*

*Guédé Nimbo,* sometimes appearing as *Baron Samedi,* personifies death itself. He is the Haitian Pluto. Dressed in black, always hungry, carrying a cross, smoking a cigar or cigarette and wearing dark glasses, *Guédé* is one of the most powerful and dreaded of the *loas.*

*Loco Attiso,* the master of the *houmfor,* and *Aïzan,* his wife, are related to *Legba.* Both are major healers and protectors against Black Magic.

*Papa 'Zaca,* or *Azzaca,* the deity of agriculture, is a crude fellow with a big appetite and the voice and proclivities of a goat. He wears a peasant's blue-denim jacket and carries a *macoute* (a market sack).

*Ogoun Feraille,* one of several powerful *Ogouns,* is the ancient patron of warriors and iron-makers. He carries a sword or machete as his symbol, and his color is red. He is often portrayed wearing a Revolutionary uniform with gold braid and epaulettes, even though he is now inclined to busy himself with politics rather than war. He corresponds with the Roman Catholic St. Jacques.

Facing page:

***Ogoun***: **God of War**
**by Antilhomme.**
**Collection, Jay Livernois, Woodstock, Connecticut**

***Ogoun***
by Hector Hyppolite.
Collection, Mr. and Mrs. Maurice C. Thompson,
Wilton, Connecticut

Let us now go more deeply into the difference between the two major branches of *vaudun*, *Rada* and *Pétro*. First of all, the deities listed above are of the *Rada* branch which are the *loas* most invoked in Haiti. *Rada* gets its name from the slaves' designation for persons abducted from Arada, on the coast of Dahomey, itself derived from the name of the holy city of the Dahomeans, Allada. Many of the slaves supplied to the Colonial French in St. Domingue (Haiti) were "Aradians" and were able to maintain their religious beliefs.

On the whole *Rada* spirits are benevolent or at least malleable. *Pétro* deities, on the other hand, while not necessarily malevolent, are definitely aggressive. Unlike the *Rada* family, they are of Haitian not African origin, and their rites (at which pigs are most often sacrificed and which are characterized by frenzy and sometimes violence) are said to have originated with a certain Dom Pèdro of Petit Goâve, a Spanish *houngan* of early Colonial times. Some see a distinct influence of Taino or Carib Amerindian rites in *Pétro cérémonies* (more likely Carib rather than Taino, since the latter were peace-loving until Columbus' slaving and gold-hungry policies turned them into fierce warriors in self-defense). Incidentally it was at a *Pétro cérémonie* in 1791 that *houngan* Boukman issued his call to bloody insurrection against the Colonial French. Other groups of *loas* which originated in other areas and tribes in West Africa (such as Ibo, Congo, etc.) are less frequently served.

The most important and unusual aspect of *vaudun* is the act of "possession" during a *cérémonie*. James Leyburn defines possession as something more than elation but less than the mystical exaltation of the enraptured saints, yet partaking of elements of both. The thing to be noted is that possession in *vaudun* occurs according to rules; participants succumbing at inappropriate times are out of order and are not treated with respect, but those seized with the *loa* being invoked, whether during the drawing of the *vever,* or in the climactic sacrifice, or during the dance that follows, are always handled with great gentleness. J.C. Dorsainvil, an *élite* (meaning a member of the wealthy Haitian mulatto class) ethnologist, regarded the *crise de possession* as abnormal, resulting in part from an historical tradition making it respectable, and in part from neurotic tendencies in the family of the person seized. But Herskovits and most other authorities since, regard possession as normal in the pattern of Haitian culture.

---

Overleaf:

**Beginning of a Possession**
by Levoy Exil.
Collection, Julia Hillman

**Metamorphosis in a Possession**
by Serge Jolimeau.
Collection, Drs. Clariel and Ingrid Antoine

The *loa* for whom the ceremony is given makes known its modest desires through the mouth of the person possessed. The latter, retaining afterwards no memory of what has happened, is relieved of anxieties by becoming the mouthpiece of an outside force. What happens to the personality during possession is conveyed in the following description by Maya Deren of two simultaneous seizures during a ceremony for *Agwé (Agoué)*:

> The initial convulsive movement occurred so suddenly that almost no one had remarked it, and now their faces, which had been normally feminine, planed off, imperceptibly, into a masculine nobility. Water was drawn up from the sea in a pail and poured over them, since normally *Agwé*, being a water divinity, would have immediately immersed himself in the *bassin*. Those who were near saluted the arrival of the divinity, and, through each of the women, *Agwé* spoke a few words of greeting in a voice which gurgled as if with rising air bubbles, and seemed truly to come from the waters. His mood was not displeased, but it was sober. The *houngan,* conscience-stricken, began to explain that he, too, would soon make a ceremony. The two *Agwés* listened to him, their eyes at once forgiving and somehow detached. And, with the same air of noble, gentle sadness, they looked slowly from person to person, from the barque of food, to the *mambo*. There was something in their regard that stilled everyone. One has seen it in the faces of those who prepare to leave and wish to remember that to which they will no longer return. They met each other's eyes, and as a way was cleared for them, approached each other, and crouched down in an embrace of mutual consolation, their arms about each other's shoulders, their foreheads lowered, each on the other's shoulder. So mirrored, they wept.[9]

The *houngan* (or *mambo* if the priest is a woman) generally inherits a calling, but to become active must serve an apprenticeship (as *La-Place* or *houngenikon* to another *houngan*), and to become influential must both demonstrate leadership in

---

[9]Deren, *op. cit.,* pp. 128-29.

the community by superior wisdom and be able to effect cures. The *houngan's* or *mambo's* symbol of authority is the *asson*, a *gourde* rattle webbed with beads and snake vertebrae to which a small bell is attached.

The *houngan's* or *mambo's* business does not stop with knowledge of the many complex rituals that must be conducted, of how to make *vevers*, or how to impart magnetism to the various participants and style to the ritual, though all of these are important.

Their equally vital function is as medical advisors to a community generally without doctors. In this capacity their knowledge of herbal remedies must be profound. As "leaf-doctors," they must know how to cure colds with infusions, shock with salt, bleeding with spider-web applications, infections with garlic. And pectin, a remedy for diarrhea, is found in the skins of many fruits. Lime juice is known to kill germs.

Michel, a Haitian boy working for our family in Jacmel one winter, had seen the pain and terror inflicted on our son when a local licensed doctor lanced his boil. When Michel suffered a similar affliction and we offered to call in the same doctor, he threatened to run away. That night he visited a *houngan* on the edge of the town and came home with a leaf attached to the ugly sore. The following morning the boil had begun to drain and subsequently healed.

A Haitian friend of ours in La Boule sprained her ankle badly. We recommended hot and cold compresses, but a local *houngan* wrapped the swollen ankle in a bandage containing leaves, and the next day it was almost normal. There is even a case of a *houngan* on La Tortue island off Port-de-Paix, who is said to have cured yaws with poultices of mold—which of course is the basis of penicillin.

When the illness is beyond their capacity, reputable *houngans* or *mambos* (it is the disreputable ones who have given this aspect of *vaudun* a bad name) will send the patient to a licensed physician. But many of the *houngan's* or *mambo's* cures are in the realm of psychosomatic medicine. The psychosomatic therapy of *vaudun* is at least as remarkable as the medicine of these natural healers. No one who has attended a genuine ceremony can have failed to notice the exhilaration and sense of well-being with which most participants leave— especially, perhaps, those who have been possessed.

Milo Rigaud describes the great lengths to which a *societé* once went to revitalize a young man struck down and near death from a disease none of the Port-au-Prince physicians could diagnose. When all else seemed to have failed, the ailing man, who had not eaten in weeks, was lowered into a hole in which a chicken had already been buried alive. A young banana tree was placed beside him (if it survived, he would die). His body was next rubbed down with flaming alcohol. He was given a clove of garlic to hold on his tongue. The *mambo* spat, then gave this invocation:

> With the permission of God, the Saints, the Dead, by the power of *Papa Brisé, Monsieur Agueroi-Linsou, Monsieur Guédé Nibo, Monsieur Guédé Nouvarou,* and all *Guédés,* I demand that you return the life of this man. I *Mambo Yabofai,* demand the life of this man. I buy for cash; I pay you; I owe you nothing!

And miraculously, after a dozen more esoteric ministrations, the young man did recover. In fact the following morning he was able to get up by himself and wash. He spoke and asked for something to eat. He was given tea and vegetable broth. For dinner he requested potato pancakes and red herring. Rigaud called his recovery "a veritable resurrection."[10]

*Houngans* and *mambos* are apt to be trusted by peasants to whom an *élite* doctor is a visitor from some hostile planet. Moreover they insist on the patients "putting themselves right" with the offended *loas* thus often contributing to the patients' peace of mind and psychic capacity to recuperate.

---

[10] Milo Rigaud, *Secrets of Voodoo,* trans. Robert B. Cross (San Francisco: City Lights Books, 1969, rpt. 1985), pp. 207-15.

In the 1930's or 1940's the average *houngans* or *mambos* were quite skilled and sincere in their belief in the power of *vaudun*. In the 1950's and later, driven out of many provincial areas by the Catholic Church and Evangelical Christian sects, the temptations for a *houngan* or *mambo* to exploit their powers commercially was strong. But an effective deterrent on the average *houngan's* or *mambo's* capacity to go astray is *vaudun's* lack of civil sanctions; communicants are free to change a *houngan* or *mambo* if they believe that they are being hoodwinked.

The savage assault on the *houmfors* in May of 1986 was at least in part a reaction to the political power vested in the *houngans* and *mambos* between 1957 and 1973 by President François ("Papa Doc") Duvalier, himself not only a *vaudouist* but also a *houngan* of *Pétro*. Under the less brutal dictatorship of his anointed successor and son that followed, things quieted down until "Baby Doc's" flight in 1986. Without the encouragement of General Namphy, who stood by and closed his eyes while Catholic and Protestant fanatics took advantage of the unarmed *houmfors,* the sway of *vaudun* would not have been threatened even temporarily.

An interesting question in relation to *vaudun* is what part sex and liquor play in *cérémonies*. The first part of this question is somewhat difficult to answer, so different are Haitian polytheistic and European monotheistic notions of what constitutes sex. In circumstances where sex is regarded as a natural and unsinful activity, where no conversational inhibitions exist, and where each of the gods as in ancient Greece and Rome is presumed to have an active marital and extra-marital sex life, it is not surprising that even the least rigid and permissive of Christian observers regard *vaudun* ceremonies as licentious. On the other hand, though occasional fertility rites are accompanied by overtly sexual acts, most ceremonies are marked by too much discipline, solemnity, and time-honored translations of act into symbol to countenance anything approaching orgies. Even the dance does not permit bodily contact; copulative movements are acted out by the dancers' hips and shoulders but never in close proximity as, say, during a waltz, tango or rumba.

As to liquor, Haitians drink, either the fiery *clairin,* or if they can afford it, the superb Barbancourt rum, in and out of *cérémonies* without any feeling of restraint, but drunkenness is rare. Alcohol is part of the life and religion of Haitians.

Another common misconception of *vaudun's* beliefs is that they somehow involve the practice of human sacrifice and/or cannibalism. *Vaudun* first acquired this reputation when Sir Spenser St. John, an English consul who despised blacks and was willing to lie to make them look uncivilized, reported the so-called Affair of Bizoton in 1863. A peasant that year had been brought to trial for allegedly sacrificing a child, and Sir Spencer promptly indicted the whole Haitian people as a nation that indulged in human sacrifice. His phrase for the alleged victim, "a goat without horns,"[11] was in turn taken over by journalists like William Seabrook—though ironically Seabrook was the first foreigner to insist that *vaudun* has as strong a claim to be considered as serious a religion as early and medieval Christianity.

Unfortunately Haitians and especially the rulers of Haiti have not always been open to or tolerant of *vaudun* as outsiders like Seabrook. Ever since Dessalines' Constitution of 1805, a law has been on the Haitian statute books prohibiting the practice of *vaudun.* Only rarely, however, has it been invoked. One such period was the time when the American Marines occupied Haiti (1915-34). So vigorously was it enforced during those years, in fact, that when Seabrook pled with Dr. Price-Mars to show him a ceremony, the Haitian scholar had to get special permission from the Commandant to "stage" one, engage a venerable *houngan* who could not find him any drums, pay him eighty dollars—and finally in-

---

[11]Sir Spenser St. John, *Hayti or The Black Republic,* (London: Smith, Elder, & Co., 1884), pp. 182-228.

formed Seabrook that it could not be managed. Seabrook's subsequent descriptions, Price-Mars said later, were based entirely on notes he showed him covering *cérémonies* that took place before the Occupation.

Under Lescot, last of the Haitian puppet-presidents put in during the American Occupation, attempts were made to re-apply the ban, and the Catholic Church was encouraged to wage a vigorous extermination campaign, burning ceremonial objects and drums, and cutting down sacred Mapou trees—but to little avail. For a while the method of controlling *vaudun* was to charge a fee of thirty dollars for any ceremony involving religious sacrifices (cocks, pigeons, goats, pigs and bulls) but considerably less for ceremonial dances alone. Clandestine *cérémonies* were hard to hide from the police and the *chefs-de-section*.This was because drumming is an essential part of all rites and the type of ceremony being held is clearly indicated by the particular rhythms used. The principal effect of that policy was to strengthen *vaudun* in and around the capital where politicians found it expedient to remain on good terms with influencial *houngans*, while weakening it in the provinces, where the Catholic Church was stronger.

The most recent attempt to proscribe *vaudun* took place under the military dictatorship of General Henri Namphy in May of 1986 when Catholic and Protestant fanatics, encour-aged by the Army which stood by, burned *vaudun* churches, *houmfors*, all over Haiti and massacred many worshippers. Not only did the assault fail, but its unprovoked brutality be-came a major factor in the expulsion of Namphy two years later. The new Constitution, ratified by the people in 1987, guarantees complete religious freedom and the protection of all religious practices.

As a result of legal protection, *vaudun cérémonies* may be held at any time, especially if an individual *serviteur* or community is in need of assistance or consolation and is willing to pay for the ritual ingredients required. However *cérémonies* are almost certain to take place on major religious holidays and saints' days, especially around Christmas; *cérémonies* during Lent are rare.

The "temple" in which the rites are held consists of an outer gathering place and one or two smaller inner chambers.The gathering place, the *péristyle* or *tonelle*, is covered with thatching or a tin roof; its center pole (the *poteau-mitan*), sometimes banded to resemble a serpent, is the "staircase" by which the *loa* enters and leaves, and around which the *vevers* (invocational designs) are drawn. Benches or chairs accommodate those not actively involved. Sometimes there is a bed to one side for the children, though any child old enough to keep awake chants and dances with its elders. The inner chamber, the *houmfor* proper, contains the altar, the drums and other ceremonial objects (though the baptized ceremonial drums are sometimes suspended when not in use from the ceiling of the *tonelle*), the earthenware jars (*govis*) or polished pre-Columbian stones (*pierres loas*) in which the ancestral spirits reside, the *houngan's* symbol of authority (*asson*), the sequined flags and bottles of the *societé*.

The best way to see a ceremony of a *societé*, especially if you do not know a Haitian who can take you to an authentic rite, is to wander about the poorer quarters of Port-au-Prince or its outskirts on a Saturday or Sunday evening. Listen for the cadence of drums and follow them. If you are not conspicuously dressed, enter the *tonelle* unobtrusively, say "Bon soir" casually to those nearest you, and behave with respect. The chances are that you will be ignored or treated courteously, and that if you wait patiently (perhaps for several hours) you may see something interesting. The *cérémonies* to which tourist agencies conduct foreigners are generally staged for that purpose. If you are on your own, and the hat is passed, give a dollar or two; if the requests are repeated, politely refuse and leave.

# *Simbi*, God of the Sweet Waters

Unlike *Agoué*, god of the salty sea, *Simbi* is the god of fresh water springs and rainfall. His symbol, a green snake in a field of crosses, indicates that he is a crossroads *loa*, with access to the heavenly waters above and the abysmal waters below. Credited with strong magic, he is the *loa* who oversees the making of the *paquet congos* (protective amulets) and *ouangas* (destructive packets). His name probably came from the *Pètro zemi* (magical thunderstones). His color is green, and he prefers the sacrifice of a speckled cock.

# CHAPTER THREE

## LA CÉRÉMONIE: RITES, DRUMS, ALTARS, FEASTS, SACRIFICES

*Voudoun* constitutes a chapter in the history of the spirit of man in the New World that is certainly no less notable, though indeed less advertised, than that of the religious imperialism of the elegantly literate slavers. Moreover, in contrast to the ironic destiny of Christianity...the function and actual effect of *Voudoun* (despised, traduced and persecuted) has been to invest the most ravaged victims of the Christian debauch with the living radiance of the timeless symbols, of which the Christian symbols themselves are but a local Near Eastern variant. Whereas God would seem to have hidden his head from the average churchgoer, to the average *serviteur* of the *hounfor* he visibly sends, even today, his angels: the gods...and man, made aware of this dimension, is in the Earthly Paradise—even where the tourist may see only a squalid heathen in a shattered hut.
—Joseph Campbell, in Maya Deren, *Divine Horsemen*

It would be convenient if a single ceremony (*cérémonie*), with all of its paraphernalia of temple, drums, altar, chants and miracles, could be described to stand for all. But ceremonies are not structured by a hierarchy. They are passed down from generation to generation, with creative compressions and additions along the way. Some, therefore, are routine, but those conducted by inspired *houngans*, are far from repetitive, and sometimes inimitable. Drama cannot be taught.

Drumming in *vaudun* is basic, since its percussions control the bodily movements of participants and its abrupt changes of rhythm and tempo bring on possession.[1] It is particularly the large *maman* which will "break"—that is change rhythm abruptly, leaving the mind in a kind of limbo and bring on a possession, or bring one out of a possession. One night after a *cérémonie* we witnessed a possessed young man staggered about, unable to come back from his state of trance. The *houngan* walked beside him, supporting him gently and asked the drummers for their help. After beating at the same tempo for a few minutes, they changed rhythm, and the young man immediately blinked awake, jerked from one world to another.

The typical battery of three drums in the *Rada* ceremony follows Dahomean prototypes. Carved from the trunk of a tree in the shape of a truncated cone, the head—of bullock or goat-skin—is stretched by means of cords attached to wooden pegs, which may then be hammered to achieve the degree of tautness required by the musician. The largest of the three drums, the *maman* (mother) is struck with the hands or a hooked wooden hammer, either on the taut drumhead or the wooden rim. Its standing drummer controls all rhythms, sometimes on signal from the *houngan* and sometimes on his own. The second drum, *segond*, is played by a musician who holds it between his legs, seated, and beats it with one hand, a forked stick or bow in the other. The smallest third drum, *bula*, is held vertically and struck with two sticks. The second and third drums provide mainly accompaniment. Sometimes a metal bell, an *ogan*, is struck with an iron rod to announce the basic rhythm which the three drums, the *maman* last, will play.

---

[1]Varying Haitian governments and hostile Christian groups attempting to suppress *vaudun* have recognized this; they go after the drums first.

Drums used in *Pètro* ceremonies are two in number, smaller than the "mother" drum used in *Rada*, their timbre controlled by crossing cords on the barrel rather than by pegs. *Pètro* rhythms and dancing are off-beat, more syncopated than in *Rada*, in keeping with the nervous tension and violence characteristic of *Pètro* ceremonies. The reader will recall that *Pètro*, though not evil, was born out of rage over the cruelties of slavery. Its rhythms echo the slave whip, and indeed the snap of an actual whip is sometimes used to accent the rhythm of the drums at moments of explosive tension. Little piles of gunpowder, ignited by a firebrand, add to the excitement during some rites.[2]

Music and dancing are important parts of all *Rada* rites, and most *Pètro* ones. Métraux calls *vaudun* a danced religion: "Dance is itself linked with divine possession—the normal mechanism by which a divinity communicates with the faithful."[3] He quotes in an English translation the text of a song intoned during a *mangé loa*:

I am making ready a meal for the Twins of Guinea
O—may they come!
I am making ready a meal, it is for the dead, a*goé*.
I am making ready a meal, it is for the Saints.

Come eat this food
*Rada, Mondongue, Don Pèdro, Mussondi, Ammine*
Come, come and eat this food,

---

[2] Maya Deren makes a point that whenever the Catholic Church has prevailed on governments to suppress *vaudun*, the *Pètro* ceremonies have become dominant. "Suppression always destroys first what is gentle and benevolent; it inspires rage and reaction, encourages malevolence and magic, and so creates the very thing which, theoretically, it would destroy." Deren, *op. cit.*, p. 62fn. The gentle, feminine *Erzulie* of *Rada* gives way to the violent *Erzulie Zérouge* (red eyes) of *Pètro*.

[3] Alfred Métraux, *Voodoo*, trans. Hugo Charteris, (New York: Oxford University Press, 1959), p. 29.

*Motokolo*, the earth is shaking, where are you?"[4]

Most songs like this one are very old and full of references to Africa, but some are topical, satirical, amusing to those familiar with the targets. This applies especially to the songs accompanying communal work in the fields, the *coumbites*.

Before describing two important ceremonies, the *mangé loa* and the *kanzo* (with its *brulé zin*) at which members of the *societé* are initiated, a word about the altar behind the *péristyle* proper. The chamber which encloses it is sometimes called the *caille-mystères*, house of the spirits. Here the holy objects are displayed for initiates. Halved and hollowed-out calabash shells, called *couis*, hold food for the hungry *loas*. There are *govis* which are lidded jars where *loas* reside when not on call. *Marassas* (twins) sometimes have platters as homes. Then there are the sacred thunderstones (polished Arawakan Taino ax-heads), rattles, playing cards, bottles of Barbancourt rum and fiery *clairin* (Haitian white-lightning made from sugarcane) used in all ceremonies by the *houngan*. Of course there are piles of costumes in a corner, should a *loa* require them: the *macoute* (knapsack) and broad-brimmed straw hat of *Papa 'Zaca*, the farmer, *Legba's* crutch, *Baron Samedi's* top-hat and cigar, *Erzulie's* cosmetics and beautiful clothes, and so on.

Doves, chickens, goats, and pigs that will be sacrificed one day are among the barnyard animals wandering about in search of food, but never allowed to starve. The *loas* would be offended by thin offerings. When they are to be sacrificed, they are chosen by the *houngan's* intuitive sense or sometimes just at random.[5]

---

[4]*Ibid.*, pp. 186-87.

[5]There is a thin line separating the painter Lafortune Félix from his other roles as *houngan* and farmer. When he paints himself holding a pig, the only clue that he is portraying himself as a farmer is that the other hand holds a shepherd's crook rather than an *asson*.

A typical *mangé loa* ceremony begins with signals to the four points of the compass by the *houngan*, holding a jug of water. There are salutations to *Legba*, without whose permission nothing can happen; to the Christian Trinity and the *vaudun* one: *Mystères, Marassas, Morts.* Libations are then offered to the *loas* from the jug, including one at the *poteau mitan* to facilitate the *loa's* descent, fireman-style.

The *houngan* is now prepared to make his *vevers* around the post. First he draws a very wide circle with chalk, ashes or flour. From this base the individual drawings appropriate to the *loas* to be summoned, radiate. The *houngan*, never kneeling or consulting any manual, carries his material in a plate, and with the other hand allows the white stuff to dribble close to the earth as he moves forward or retreats. If he is skillful, with a wide repertoire of symbolic signs, the *vevers* of the various spirits to be offered food are astonishingly intricate and beautiful—though destined to be obliterated once the dancing begins. Only thanks to instant flash-photography can the heart of *Erzulie*, the ship of *Agoué*, the serpents of *Damballah* and *Aida-Wedo*, be appreciated by those not present to see them created.

In any case, the time has now come for the *hounsis*, bearing sequined ceremonial flags, to back in, then turn and curtsy as they approach the central post. There they kneel, kiss the ground, and salute the *houngan* with his gourde rattle and saber, and whatever visiting dignitaries may be present. The chants, Roman Catholic litanies, and *priéres Guinèe* (sacred songs) which follow, to appropriate drum rhythms, may in some instances consume hours. But for the feasting of the *loa*, the ceremony most frequently performed in Haiti, they are essential. Since there is no refrigeration in peasant Haiti, farm animals must be killed immediately before they are cooked. "This does not mean that the chickens, goats, pigs to be sacrificed, are killed 'in cold blood.' On the contrary," Maya Deren points out, "in the course of being ritualistically prepared, the animal enjoys more tenderness and care than one destined for purely secular purposes. While this could not be understood to 'console' the animal, it does make evident to one who has observed it, the fact that the Haitian is completely innocent of any brutal emotion or intention toward it."[6] On the day of the sacrifice the animal is given a purifying bath. Goats are "dressed" with elaborate ribbons on their horns and draped with silk handkerchiefs, and shortly before sacrifice, their beards are cut, and they are castrated. Bulls to be sacrificed may wear elegant robes and be led about the *houmfor* grounds communing with the trees in which the spirits are believed to live (*arbres-reposoirs*).

Doves or chickens, the commonest sacrifices, are killed for *Rada* deities with a twist of the neck, for *Pètro* with a slit throat. The blood is used to anoint sacred objects or make crosses on the foreheads of each *serviteur*. The dead animal is then laid upon the *vever*. After its entrails have been offered to the *loa*, the body is cleaned and later eaten. But before this the animal about to be sacrificed is offered food from a sacramental dish. If it eats, it is believed that the *loa* has accepted the proposed sacrifice. If it does not eat, the *loa* has rejected the animal, and it is allowed to go free. *Houngans* take birds by their feet and brush their feathers lightly across the faces of all the faithful, an action strangely thrilling to the recipient. Through this act each participant shares in the sacrifice and in the benevolence which comes from the pleased gods.

Possession (*crise de possession*), on the part of a *hounsi* or other participant or even spectator, is most likely to occur at the moment of sacrifice. The abruptly shifting drum rhythms pile climax on climax. Consciousness, in the balance, yields to the *loa*. What is said or done by the possessed is never known (until released by the *loa*). For the possessed, the *cheval* (horse), whom the *loa* has chosen to "mount" changes even physically while possessed, his gestures, expressions, voice being those of the *loa*, not of the unpossessed self. "An

---

[6]Deren, *op. cit.*, pp. 213-14.

eight year-old child mounted by a *Grande* (an older woman *mystère*) such as *Grande Erzulie*, will be feeble, practically speechless, and speaking like a woman a hundred years old; while an old man of ninety possessed by a raging *Ogoun* such as *Bacossou* will bound out of his torpor, brandish his sword, and dance better than Nureyev."[7] Some older people, forced by the inhabiting *loa* to excessive exertion, may afterwards have to spend days in bed recuperating. People who do not know how to swim, when possessed by *Agoué*, move like Olympians. One woman whose boat capsized would have drowned had *Agoué* not possessed her and showed her body how to swim to shore. The coquettish *Erzulie* often speaks in elaborate French although her *cheval* has never spoken a word of it and comprehends nothing but Créole. These are a few of *vaudun's* miracles.

*Kanzo*, the initiation rite that every true believer must submit to, is a grueling experience. Métraux is right to stress the financial sacrifice, absence from one's life-sustaining occupation, efforts of memory, acceptance of strict discipline and moral obligation which the initiate must assume. "*Kanzo*," he says, "makes for a more direct contact with the divinity. It also acts as a guarantee against the tricks of fate, bad luck, and above all, illness...Thanks to these rites initiates not only ensure for themselves a supernatural ally, but also steep themselves in beneficent effluvia. *Kanzo* 'gives you a *nanm*' (soul). Some of the rites have an entirely magical nature and even though superficially they may appear to be tests of endurance and courage, in fact their real function is to increase the luck and health of the novice."[8]

Sometimes—one can never be sure that the ceremony or ceremonies one has seen are the characteristic ones—the *kanzo* begins even before the initiate arrives. He (or more likely she)—for most initiates go to all this trouble and expense in

---

[7]Rigaud, *op. cit.*, p. 46.
[8]Métraux, *op. cit.*, p. 193.

order to become accredited *hounsis*—takes a purifying bath, eats sparingly, and drinks a concoction of *corrosál*, the fruit that looks like a hand grenade and is supposed to have a sedative effect. Now comes the *chiré aïzan*, in which dried palm fronds are torn into strips, and worn as *gardes* (protection) against evil spirits. The next step is the *coucher* (putting-to-bed) with the initiates lying down like spokes of a wheel around the *poteau mitan*, there to be sometimes whipped across the legs; lectures by the *houngan* or *mambo* about the seriousness of what one is about to experience and one's obligations.

The initiates are then ushered, sometimes not too gently, into the chamber where they may be locked up for as long as a week. What goes on there is supposed to be a secret, but the novices are certainly clad in white, shaved everywhere except on the head from which a lock of hair has been cut to join their nail-parings. The *lavé-tête* which follows prepares the novice for the particular *loa* to whom he or she will be consecrated. Which *loa*? The one whose "horse" the initiate had been in a first possession, or lacking that guidepost, by any *loa* deemed appropriate by the chief priest.

The sequined flags and *govis* are now carried in, the *vevers* are drawn, and each novice lies on a mat close to his or her sign of choice. Doves or chickens to be sacrificed are brought in, have their wings and legs broken (to appropriate drum rhythms) and sometimes the *houngan* tears out the bird's tongue with his teeth before breaking its neck, anointing each novice's forehead with three drops of blood. Any initiate not already possessed by this time, is certain to be when his or her *loa* is called by name. The *loa* inhabiting the possessed novice, is now free to eat—and sometimes gorges himself or herself after the long fast.

Seen as a symbolic rite of death and resurrection, the initiate is now ready to undergo the final test of *kanzo*, the trial by fire, or *brulé-zin*. Draped in a white sheet, or covered with one so that no part of the head or body may be seen, the initiate receives a handful of boiling meal which the *houngan* himself has seized from the *zin* (pot), taking it in his hand. The hot gruel is returned to the *zin* by the novice, his or her feet pass over the flame, and the entire procedure is repeated at each *brulé-zin*. If the *zin* is of clay, it cracks from the heat, and is buried, along with its contents in a hole lined with leaves.

The following morning, the novices (who are no longer novices) re-enter the "real" world, clad in white, wearing their masks of palm-leaves honoring *Aïzan*. They are led forth still under their white sheets to visit the sacred trees surrounded by necklaces of stones and salute their spirits. They are then free to re-enter the *péristyle* where a dance in their honor is generally held.

Milo Rigaud, who is the foremost Haitian expert on *vaudun*, describes a sacrifice of a bull to *Simbi* that we witnessed with him at a *houmfor* in Croix-des-Bouquets in 1960. Since the ceremony was of the *Pètro* variety, red brick-dust was added to the other ingredients—powder, flour, ashes—with which the *houngan* Dieucifor had already drawn an assortment of beautiful *vevers* around the *poteau-mitan*. (*Simbi* would be accompanied by other *loas* and none of them could be neglected with impunity).

To the clang of an iron *ogan*, the *hounsis* began to enter the *péristyle*. A big ceremonial whip was unfastened from the post and cracked furiously in the courtyard to the accompaniment of strident whistle blasts. A jug of water, lighted candles, and *couis* containing a mixture of cornmeal and roasted peanuts, were added to the other foods and drinks for the *loas* already assembled on a large table.

The sacrificial animals—goats wearing red-satin foulards amid their bell-hung horns, cocks and doves—had been appropriately bathed, and now joined the black bull tethered to a post and adorned with a snowy mantle and red ribbons.

Facing page:

Drawing of a *vever* for a bull sacrifice to *Simbi*
Photo, Selden Rodman, 1959.[9]

**The Sacrifice of the Cock**
by Wilson Bigaud, 1954.
Collection, the Authors

---

[9] This is a photo of the drawing of the *vever* for the bull sacrifice described in the following pages which the authors witnessed along with Milo Rigaud. The artist André Pierre acted as *La-Place* during this ceremony.

The *hounsis'* first chant honors the house. The second is addressed to *Legba* who will make way for the flags and protect the other *loas*. While the houngan consecrates the *vevers* with holy water (Florida water!) and salutations, the sequined flags are brought out of the inner chamber along with the ritual sword. It will take more than a machete-chop to drop a beast as noble as this—unless they resort to butchery, but grace not butchery is the *vaudun* way.

Prayers, chants, litanies in the Roman Catholic style consume more than an hour, following which the houngan returns to those great abstract drawings of his—can he be yielding to aesthetic pride? He would never admit it, of course, and we knew better than to suggest such a thing to a scholarly purist like our companion to whom Maya Deren, a purist in her own way, had introduced us to almost reverently. In any event the *houngan* does what he is expected to do, placing little piles of grain here and there and sprinkling libations, for hungry *loas* can be thirsty too. Small pyramids of gunpowder are ignited with a flaming stick as the drum rhythms syncopate abruptly, bringing on the first possessions. The whole assemblage cries out in unison *"Adjioh! Adjioh!"* and then the next song breaks out loud and clear:

> *Caille moin, senti foulah,*
> *O Toutou Bilango.*
> *Macaya, m'senti foulah.*
> *Trois feuilles, Trois points,*
> *M'senti foulah!*
> *Toutou Bilango.*
> *Caille , O caille ,*
> *Caille moin senti foulah,*
> *Toutou Bilango!*

> My house, feels the spray,
> Oh, *Toutou Bilango.*
> *Macaya,* I feel the spray.
> Three leaves, Three points,
> I feel the spray!

*Toutou Bilango.*
Oh, house, Oh house, Oh,
My house feels the spray,
*Toutou Bilango!*[10]

The house "felt the spray," the spirit, as did we all. So did *Macaya, Three Leaves,* and *Three Points,* all identifiable minor *loas,* but did *Toutou Bilango?* The name haunted us then and still does. Who was he? A *loa?* An identifiable person, historic or contemporary? Or one long-forgotten except in this one chant? We never found out. *Toutou Bilango...*

Dieucifor seizes the bottle of alcoholic *kimanga* and vaporizes it between his teeth. To the north, to the west, to the south, to the east. The drums roll menacingly. Visiting *mambos* present him with the sacrificial birds, passing them over his limbs lightly. Suddenly he grabs birds, breaks their wings and feet, tears our their tongues with his teeth, and then kills them swiftly with a sharp knife, consecrating their blood to the appropriate *loas.* A woman is possessed. Her voice is deep-throated: she is a male *loa.* The *hounsis* scatter. To an augmented whip-cracking and whistle-blowing outside, the two goats are brought in. They are used to the noise by now. They stand there quietly munching Guinea grass, oblivious to their imminent sacrifice.

Without warning they are seized by their feet and swung high overhead while the singers and drummers go wild, others chant:

*Koumba cabrite télékou é.*
*Koumba, koumba cabrite, télékiou é,*
*Cabrite télékou...*[11]

The animals are thrown on their backs. A cross is drawn on each with a sharp knife. They are castrated, blood from the

---

[10]Rigaud, *op. cit.,* p. 199.
[11]Rigaud, *op. cit.,* p. 203.

severed testicles falls on the *vevers*. They are dispatched with quick knife-thrusts to the neck, the blood carefully collected in bowls and deposited along with the lifeless bodies on the ritual drawings.

Almost immediately the bull is brought in, but proves much harder to handle. He shakes loose from his guides, swerves, and butts the center post so fiercely the whole *tonelle* shudders. Several daring young men (possessed by *Simbi*) leap on the bull's back and ride him quite successfully. Applause encourages them. Will everyone be possessed? The *houngan* is not pleased. He hobbles the bull with rope thongs and has him led outside for a calming circuit of the yard.

"Why?" We ask Milo.

"He is probably afraid that things could get out of hand."

"That a sacred ceremony could turn into a bullfight?"

He smiles but does not answer directly. "People could be injured," he says. "The police might intervene and prohibit ceremonies to come."

Whatever the reasons, the bull is brought back in and slain with a skillful sword thrust behind the neck and into the heart, falling to its knees—just as in a bullring! But those who have never visited a Latin country—everyone present except us, no doubt—are unperturbed. Religion has prevailed. The excitement soon drains away. The drumming subsides to a few long rolls, punctuated by silences. There is a final chant, a final prayer. The ceremony is over.

### Marriage to a *Loa*

A *cérémonie*, less common because of its expense, is the marriage of a human to a *loa*. It most often occurs when a man or woman who has been especially devoted to a *loa*, decides to make a human marriage and fears the *loa's* jealousy. The devotee may decide to marry the *loa* first in order to avert supernatural anger and danger to his spouse. *Erzulie*, because of her coquetry and jealousy, is the *loa* most likely to demand marriage, but marriages to *Ogoun, Damballah,* and *Guédé* also occur.

Conducted like a bourgeois wedding with all the trimmings—white gown, veil, and flowers; wedding suit and satin shirt; cake and champagne for the whole community—such weddings can be as costly as the income of the bride or groom allows.

When a human marriage is to follow, the person entering into marriage with a *loa* always hopes that the *loa* will choose to possess his fiancé and use that person as the *cheval* (horse) during the *cérémonie,* but *loas* are capricious and may enter anyone present, even a member of the wrong sex. A woman betrothed to *Ogoun,* for instance, may find herself marrying another woman who has been possessed by him. Indeed, the *loa* may even decide to possess his own bride, which would mean the placing of both marriage rings on the same finger.

The *cérémonie* begins with the traditional drumming, and the chanting of both voodoo and Catholic litanies, led by a *père savanne* (bush priest).[12] When the *loa* arrives and makes his presence known by possessing someone present, that person is rushed off to be dressed in the bridal attire. Then the pair take their vows, exchange rings and sign the marriage contract prepared by the *père savanne.* The bridal couple is congratulated by the community, the wedding cake is cut, and a reception of feasting and dancing follows. Any person married to a *loa* must set aside several nights of the week for the spirit. To cohabit with a human on the *loa's* night would constitute adultery.

---

[12]An unordained rural Catholic priest.

## Ceremony of *Retirer d'en bas de l'eau*[13]

When a person has been dead for a year and a day, the family may choose to reclaim the soul from the abysmal waters and place it in a *govi* on the family altar where it can be consulted when family decisions are made. Because the *cérémonie*, too, is expensive, the community may wait to conduct it until many families join together to bring back their honored dead. Some souls are thus forced to wait for long periods of time and may take vengeance on their uncaring families by causing illness and disaster.

A trough of water is placed in the *péristyle* to symbolize the waters of the abyss. It is covered by a white sheet, set up like a tent. After the drumming has begun, a procession of white-robed *hounsis,* carrying empty *govis* on their heads, enters from the altar chamber and proceeds to the trough, where each lies down, extending her head with the *govi* toward the tent. The *hounsis* must walk and lie on straw mats for it is feared that should they touch the earth, unwanted spirits might enter the jars.

Within the tent, the *houngan* exhorts the souls to come forth, while the *houngenikon* leads songs of greeting. The sound of the sacred *asson,* with its rattling shells and ringing bell is heard, as the *houngan* calls out the names of the souls to be recalled. Finally the voices of the dead themselves resound, and each *hounsi* is convulsed as the *govi* on her head is filled. Often souls who are not being called, cry piteously, asking their families to bring them back. Some souls arrive in anger and are difficult for the *houngan* to handle. Some arrive joyfully and are greeted by members of their families with rejoicing and tears. Some arrive spitefully and divulge embarrassing family secrets to the assembled community.

---

[13]Although the source of this *cérémonie* has not yet been verified, it seems that it originated in the Congo. A *Santería* priest we interviewed in Puerto Rico told us he had witnessed such a ceremony in the Congo when he visited Africa in search of the origins of *Santería* rituals.

When all of the *govis* have been filled, the assembly is entitled to a celebration of feasting and dancing, but often the *cérémonie* has been so long and harrowing, all are tired and wish only to take their soul-filled *govis* and go home.

---

# *Damballah*, God of Fertility

*Damballah* is the Cosmic snake from whose egg the world was hatched. Thus he is the source of new life, the mystic power of regeneration and birth. Together with his wife, *Aida-Wedo,* the rainbow, he rules the sky. Those possessed by him climb trees, writhe in accessible waters, and hiss. His color is white and his favorite food, an egg.

# CHAPTER FOUR

## SYNCRETISM

The reason the Catholic Church in Haiti finds itself in the often helpless position of trying to convert the already converted, is that *vaudun*, an adaptable cult without written codes or any country-wide hierarchy of its own, has managed to integrate into its structure almost all the symbols, ceremonies and outward forms of the Roman Church. The Saints have been melded with the African deities (*loas*), who were also sometimes once human beings. The Cross of Christ doubles for the sign of *Baron Samedi*, and also for the symbol of the treacherous crossroads, guarded over by the African god *Legba*. Baptism is an old African tradition pre-dating Christianity. And no one who has seen in Haiti the once-Catholic rites of Ash Wednesday (Mardi Gras) and Lent (*Ra-Ra*) will deny that it is the *serviteurs* of *vaudun* who have adapted them to their own ends. The Holy Trinity is thought by some to correspond roughly to the three primitive powers invoked at all *vaudun* rites, *les Mystères, les Morts, les Marassas* (the Spirits, the Dead, the Twins). The Almighty Himself (*le Bon Dieu, Grand Maître*) is recognized as having precedence over the *loas* but, as God, is believed to be too busy to concern himself with mundane trivia.

> Don't the Catholic and the *Vodun* worshipper believe in the exis-
> tence of a supreme God? Don't they both believe in His unceas-
> ing intervention in the course of human life as well as in the
> realm of universal phenomena? Don't they believe Him sensitive
> to offense, terrible in vengeance and yet merciful, responsive to
> prayer and to offerings of his poor creatures lost in misery and
> sin? Don't they believe in supernatural beings—saints, angels
> and demons—who stand between man and his Creator and are
> ever disposed to concern themselves with the  affairs of this
> world?[1]

The differences between Catholicism and *vaudun* are fundamental, of course, but not easy to define.

> "To serve the *loa* you have to be a Catholic..." These words—of
> a Marbial peasant—deserve to stand as epigraph to this chapter
> for they express, very precisely, the paradoxical ties between
> Voodoo and Christianity.[2]

Flying from Port-au-Prince to New York one day, we were
seated beside an elderly Haitian woman who clutched a
French language edition of the *Bible* and proceeded to read it
from the moment the plane left the ground.

Our children, Carla and Van, then aged eight and ten, were
bored on the flight, so in order to amuse them, we produced
some paper so they could draw *vevers*. When the Haitian
woman saw what they were doing, her eyes bulged with fear.
"Don't let them do that!" she admonished in French. "Those
signs are evil; they are bad; drawing them is dangerous!"

We calmed her as well as we could and asked why she was
so upset by the *loa*. "I used to go to *cérémonies* all the time,"
she said, "and I was always afraid." Raising her *Bible*, she as-

---

[1]Jean Price-Mars, *So Spoke the Uncle,* trans. Magdaline Shannon, (Three
Continents Press, 1983), p. 154.
[2]Métraux, *op. cit.*, p. 323.

serted, "Now I have a stronger god who protects me from them."

Perhaps some people thought this woman had been converted, but this really wasn't so. She still believed in the African deities, still feared their power.

Métraux says that the clergy was often amazed

> ...by mass conversions of Voodooists who, seized by a vague collective enthusiasm, "abjured" in large numbers and came flocking to the priests, asking them to destroy the ritual objects which they possessed and to "free them from the impossible obligations which had been imposed on them." The "obligations" which Voodoo imposes on its devotees explain in many cases the ease with which many of them abjured and the enthusiasm they showed—probably to cover secret misgivings.[3]

> Many Voodooists have become Protestants not because Voodoo failed to supply their need for a purer, loftier religion, but on the contrary, because they felt themselves to be the target of angry *loa* and saw in Protestantism a refuge. Hence Protestantism beckons as though it were a shelter, or more precisely a magic circle, where people cannot be got at by *loa* and demons. Conversion, far from being the result of a *crise de conscience*, is often no more than the expression of an exaggerated fear of the spirits. The role of Protestantism among Voodooists was well defined to me in a saying which I heard in Marbial and quote here word for word: "If you want the *loa* to leave you in peace— become a Protestant.[4]"

Most Haitians, to be on the safe side, pay their respects to both religions. Even the *élite*, who may never go to a *houm-for,* have heard about the *loa* in the cradle, while rocked by their lower class servants. In time of trouble these people will often seek the aid of a *bocor* or *houngan.*

Such was true of the artist, Ramphis Magloire, who suffered a nervous breakdown when the Duvaliers' departure left Haiti

---

[3]*Ibid.*, pp. 351-52.
[4]*Ibid.*, p. 342.

in total chaos. Although every member of his family was an avowed Protestant, his brother, Stivenson, suggested that perhaps Ramphis should consult the *houngan* of Petit Trou de Nippes, where their mother Louisianne St. Fleurant (also a famous artist) had been born.

Ramphis, accordingly, made the trip from his home in Pétion-Ville to the little town on the south peninsula in search of a "cure." The *houngan* announced that the family gods were indeed angry for no one had "fed" them for many, many years. After Ramphis had paid for the ceremonial necessities and presided over the sacrifice of a rooster, he felt better. He returned to Port-au-Prince, his equilibrium restored, and began to paint in a completely new style.

It could be argued that political events had caused the artist's anxiety, but *vaudun*, nonetheless, provided an effective cure. By taking action in placating the gods, Ramphis believed he was again in control of his life and could continue with his work regardless of the chaos around him.

The *pé*, or sacred altar, in every *houmfor*, is a strange mixture of Catholic and *vaudun* elements. Almost always the central image of the god will be a "borrowed" Catholic lithograph. If the shrine honors *Erzulie*, an image of the Virgin Mary, wearing her blue scarf, will preside. If it is *Ogoun*, a picture of St. Jacques will be riding his white horse, carrying a sword and brandishing the Haitian national flag. *Damballah*, the snake god, will be represented by St. Patrick, *Azacca*, the god of agriculture, by St. Isadore. *Agoué*, the Haitian Poseidon, is seen as St. Ulrique because this saint is usually seen holding a fish, while *Legba*, the African Hermes, can be identified with either St. Lazarus or St. Anthony the Hermit.

Before each image in the *houmfor* will be a bowl of cornmeal in the *vaudun* tradition, candles as on a Catholic altar, and often magical thunder stones so prized by Amerindians. *Erzulie* will be flanked by perfumes, jewelry, make-up, and mirrors, and *Ogoun* by swords, flags, and implements made of iron. Also present will be a number of *govi* and *pots-de-tête*, believed to contain the souls of the *loas* and the *hounsis*.

The *vaudun* service itself is permeated with many prayers and hymns of Christian origin. Latin words may be interspersed in the *langage* used to call the spirits. The *houngan* begins the *cérémonie* by reciting Paters, Confiteors, and Ave Marias, followed by hymns to the Virgin and the Saints. And *vaudun* has not only appropriated the use of holy water, but also *bocors* often force their customers to steal the wafer from the Catholic communion because of its magical properties.

The Christmas season elicits a great deal of activity in the *houmfor,* and many special *cérémonies* are scheduled. Ritual baths are often given to ensure good health and good luck, and special pilgrimages to sacred caves or springs are often held at this holy time.

During the week preceding Easter, *vaudun* images are often covered with cloths like the statues in a Catholic church. The famous *vaudun* pilgrimage to Saut-d'Eau, held every July, so that *serviteurs* can bathe in the waterfall sacred to the Haitian water god, *Simbi,* now has Christian overtones, for a nearby chapel, built to honor St. John and the Virgin, receives the same devotees.

The strong Amerindian component in the *Pètro* branch of *vaudun* has generally been ignored, largely because scholars interested in *vaudun* have been Africanists, eager to search for sources only on the Dark Continent in order to prove the religion "pure" African. Maya Deren, however, has made a powerful argument for the consideration of Amerindian influences.[5]

The Taino and Carib Amerindians, who were the original inhabitants of Haiti, believed that the souls of their ancestors resided in thunder stones, which they called *zemi. Zemi* was also the Taino word for soul, and the word is still used in *vaudun* for these same stones and other magical objects be-

---

[5]Deren, *op. cit.*, pp. 61-71.

lieved to have great powers. And linguistically related to *zemi*, is *Simbi*, the name of the fresh water god; *Baron Samedi*, the god of the cemetery; and *zombie*, a body deprived of its soul.

*Azacca*, or *Papa 'Zaca*, the god of agriculture, has never been traced to Africa. His name may come from *zara*, the Amerindian word for corn, from *azada*, their word for hoeing, or from a group of *maza*-structured words from which the word maize is derived.

The *asson*, the sacred rattle of the *houngan*, is recorded in Taino myth, and priests in the Amazon always carried such a symbol of authority. In Africa such rattles are used solely as musical instruments and not for religious purposes. Its beaded decoration is surely of Amerindian derivation.

No traces of the *Guédés*, spirits of the cemetery, of whom *Baron Samedi* is chief, have been found in Africa, and in Haitian *cérémonies* they are always treated apart. The living dead of the Caribs were known to walk about at night (like zombies), to love tobacco (like Baron Samedi), and to have problems with their eyes (the *Guédés* always wear sunglasses). The Amerindians, who had come to the islands from the mainland, were known to have contacts with the Mayan, Inca, and Aztec civilizations. *Guédés* always come out and cavort on November 1st, while in Mexico, November 1st is the Day of the Dead.

Many of the *Pètro* gods are called *ze rouge* (with red eyes); it was a common practice for Caribs to paint their faces, especially their eyes, in order to appear fierce. A *baka* is a red-eyed animal believed to be a demon; in the Yucatan a *bacab* is a spirit with an animal or human head. Carib women were known to wear leg bands below the knee, and such bands are tied around the arms and legs of all participants in *Pètro cérémonies*.

The most obvious accretion in the New World is the use of *vevers*, kabbalah-like designs drawn on the floor with flour or cornmeal to call the gods. These designs do not exist in Africa and have a strong resemblance to the sand paintings made by Amerindians on both American continents. Fearful that the master would discover wooden icons and punish them for practicing their outlawed religion, African slaves may have searched for a more "disposable" image. Thus they would have welcomed the sand-painting technique of the few surviving Caribs and Tainos who had run into the hills temporarily escaping from Spanish slavery and genocide. Certainly these images were constantly changed and refined by the African *houngan*-artists, who used their fertile imaginations to apply visual elements from their own environment. The curlicues and embellishments strongly resemble the elaborate ironwork then being installed on the homes of their French and Spanish masters.

Finally, it is acknowledged that the *Pètro* cult was founded by a "Latin" *houngan* named Dom Pèdro. Since he spoke Spanish it is likely he was an Amerindian, for they, and not Africans, comprised most of the slaves during the early Spanish period.

## *Aïzan,* Healer and Protector

*Aïzan,* the first priestess, and her husband, *Loco,* are the heterosexual aspects of *Legba,* who is often thought of as androgynous. As the mother of spiritual life, she is the protector of the *houmfor* and the guardian of the ceremonies. Her sign, the palm leaf, is used to cover the faces of the initiates, and her association with plant life makes her the expert in herbal cures. Her colors are white and silver. Since she presides over the ceremonies, she never possesses anyone.

# CHAPTER FIVE

## *VAUDUN* AS INSPIRATION: THE ARTS IN HAITI

From its inception in 1945, popular art in Haiti was dominated by *vaudun*. It began with the discovery of Hector Hyppolite, a *houngan* from St. Marc who had struck bottom that year both as a priest and as an artist.[1] Fortunately for him—and for Haitian art—Hyppolite had just painted floral decorations with a brush of chicken feathers on the doors of a roadside bar with the prophetic name *Ici La Renaissance*. The doors were glimpsed in Mont Rouis by DeWitt Peters and Philippe Thoby-Marcelin on their way to Cap Haitien. Peters was an American water-colorist who had had a wartime assignment in Haiti to teach English and had just opened *Le Centre d'Art*, hoping to arouse Haitian interest in the arts—up to now a backwater of French academicism. His companion was a Haitian novelist about to achieve fame for his satirical stories of Haitian life.[2] On their way back the two friends stopped and asked who had painted the doors. Encountering

---

[1]Hyppolite was living in poverty in St. Marc, having lost his flock when he decided to pursue art rather than religion. Or so he told us.

[2]This novel is *Canapé Vert*, by Philippe Thoby-Marcelin and Pierre Marcelin, published by Farrar & Rinehart in 1944.

Hyppolite nearby, they had little difficulty persuading the *houngan* to receive a gift of primed cardboard and cans of Sapolin furniture enamel.

In a few days Hyppolite visited the *Centre* with his first completed pictures; his career as a painter began. The largest of his pictures was born aloft and carried through the streets of the capital in triumph,[3] making Peters think back to similar happenings in Quattrocento Florence. Peters paid the *houngan* and when a second batch of paintings arrived, visitors from abroad, including André Breton, the ideologue of Surrealism, and the Cuban modernist painter, Wifredo Lam, bought six of the little pictures and took them to Paris. At an exhibition there sponsored by UNESCO, they created a sensation. Paintings taken and exhibited in New York received as much acclaim.

Hyppolite told me in 1947 that he had traveled in Africa years before with an unemployed artist he had met in the cane fields of Cuba, and that he had supported himself on his travels by painting flowers on chamber pots. Whether that voyage really took place anywhere but in Hyppolite's vivid imagination, there was no doubt of his sense of mission. And the credulous can even see a resemblance to the Coptic wall paintings of Ethiopia in Hyppolite's slant-eyed Madonnas.

Hyppolite's early slap-dash paintings were not always successful but at their best they shocked with that personal flair great artists have always had. From Giotto to Rembrandt, from Manet to Picasso, every innovator in painting has had that flair from his earliest efforts. Hyppolite's subject matter—though he did later paint occasional still-lifes, portraits and nudes—was *vaudun*. Some of these pictures celebrated the *loas* he had seen in "possessions;" others owed their flights of fancy to black magic, always thereafter a stimulant to the wilder fantasies of Haitian art.

---

[3]Hyppolite's painting carried aloft in triumph depicted the apotheosis of the Virgin (or *Erzulie,* as you choose).

Peters offered Hyppolite a substantial concrete home in Port-au-Prince, but the artist was canny enough to realize that he must not separate himself from his roots. So instead he set up shop in a thatched hut, a *caille,* on the teeming waterfront, nailing a bold sign *Ici Station Peintures* above his doorway. There he lived for the next three years with his many mistresses, had a fishing smack[4] built for him, and painted up a daily storm. The six to eight hundred paintings Hyppolite created during the tragically short three year career that followed,[5] have since found their ways into the collections of major museums, private collections and auctions where they bring prices in five and six figures.

The art of other talented Haitians of the first generation took off in surprising directions while Hyppolite was still alive. Rigaud Benoit, whose mordant eye for bourgeois foibles was as sharp as Breughel's, had driven the *Centre d'Art*'s jeep and had painted mural decorations on its sides. But he was so wary of the miracle of American appreciation, he deposited his first pictures at the *Centre d'Art* under an assumed name. He and Hyppolite loved to attend American movies together, and later, Rigaud married Hyppolite's daughter. Peters' houseboy from Jacmel, Castera Bazile, had by now turned his compassionate eye on the miseries and glories of peasant existence: paintings which are sympathetic hymns to peasant tribulations and dreams. Wilson Bigaud, a boy who had helped Hyppolite keep his canvases and brushes in order at La Saline, observed the life around him with a realist's eye and later put his observations into the largest of the tempera murals in Ste. Trinité Cathedral.[6]

---

[4]A kind of boat.

[5]We have no medical report on Hyppolite's death, but we are sure it was from a combination of the usual Haitian ailments: malnutrition, dysentery, malaria and syphilis.

[6]By the time I (Selden Rodman) became co-director of the *Centre d'Art* in 1947, I had convinced Peters that the artists were ready to move from

Another artist of the first generation, Jasmin Joseph, had been discovered by Peters' assistant in sculpture, Jason Seeley, while making small figurines in clay at a foundry near Arcahaie. Joseph became Haiti's first important sculptor, and he dedicated his fired clay choir screen in the Ste. Trinité Cathedral to the memory of his friend Hector Hyppolite, who died before the great murals there got under way.

The dominant artist of the second generation, which dates from the time the tempera murals in the Cathedral were completed in 1951, was André Pierre. Pierre was a *La-Place* and later on a *houngan* who had a *houmfor* in Croix-des-Missions, across the first bridge on the road to Cap Haitien. Pierre had already painted powerful images of the *loas* on the walls of his *houmfor's* sanctuary, and, fifteen miles east in the out buildings of the largest *vaudun* temple in Haiti, he had painted more. In 1951, Maya Deren, the anthropologist and experimental filmmaker, who was then residing in the Croix-des-Missions *houmfor,* and Nancy Heinl, co-author of a book on Haitian history, persuaded Pierre to try his hand at "easel" pictures. Since he had already painted the curved inner shells of giant calabashes (used as receptacles in the *mangé loas*), his first four-sided pictures retained an oval border. For a time Pierre, like Hyppolite before him, was persuaded to move into more "bourgeois" quarters—in his case the gallery of his first dealer, Issa el Saieh in Pacot. But again, like Hyppolite, he had the good sense to return to *vaudun* and the peasant life that nurtured it. To this day he paints in a tiny thatched *caille* near the *houmfor,* though most of his paintings

the small pictures tourists could handle to the immovable walls of public buildings. It became instantly apparent through trial runs at the *Centre* that the self-taught among the artists, and they alone, were equipped to do what the so-called primitives had done during Italy's Quattrocento. The resulting murals by eight Haitian painters in the apse and transepts of the Episcopal Cathedral of Ste. Trinité, which I superintended in 1949-51, spoke louder than print shirts and were soon reproduced worldwide.

are now commissioned by collectors in Germany, France and the United States. There, fortified by a bottle of *clairin,* he turns out canvases richly colorful but without much inventive variation.

André Pierre's paintings always depict the *loas* of *vaudun* in the costumes of the Colonial period—*Ogoun* in the uniform of a general, *Agoué* as an admiral rising from the sea, *Brigitte-La-Croix* in billowing purple robes, *La Sirène* as a mermaid, *Baron Samedi* with his black cross, top hat and cigar.

This was true of most other major artists of the second generation. Wilmino Domond of Marbial and Préfèt Duffaut of Civadier painted the local *loas* in their highly personal styles. The *Reine Titane* was Duffaut's favorite *loa,* and in the first mural I commissioned him to paint in Ste. Trinité Cathedral, he painted a processional with tiny figures circling steep mountains on their way to a cross. In the second mural he painted Christ on the temple's pinnacle exactly as he had *Erzuli* on her mountain top. Another great painter from southern Haiti of the Jacmel area, Pauléus Vital, zeroed in on *magie noire,* his scenes of diabolical happenings generally taking place in underground grottoes.

Gérard Valcin, a tile-setter in the capital, also painted *vaudun* inspired pictures—*cérémonies* on off-shore islands with cakes being thrown to crocodiles and big fish were his specialty. White-robed *hounsis* swaying rhythmically against black and white tiles were also effective.

Two other painters of the second generation, Enguérrand Gourgue and Célestin Faustin roamed further afield in their styles. Gourgue had painted his first picture, a sensational "Magic Table" in the late 1940's while still a teenager; it became the first Haitian painting to be acquired by the Museum of Modern Art in New York. Moving to larger and more ambitious pictures of *vaudun* and *magie noire,* Gourgue lived in Spain in the 1960's and 1970's where he perfected his already formidable technique and acquired a world-wide clientele of collectors.

---

Facing page:

**Guédé as Revolutionary General**
by André Pierre, 1952.
Present Whereabouts Unknown

**Erzulie**
by Célestin Faustin.
Private Collection

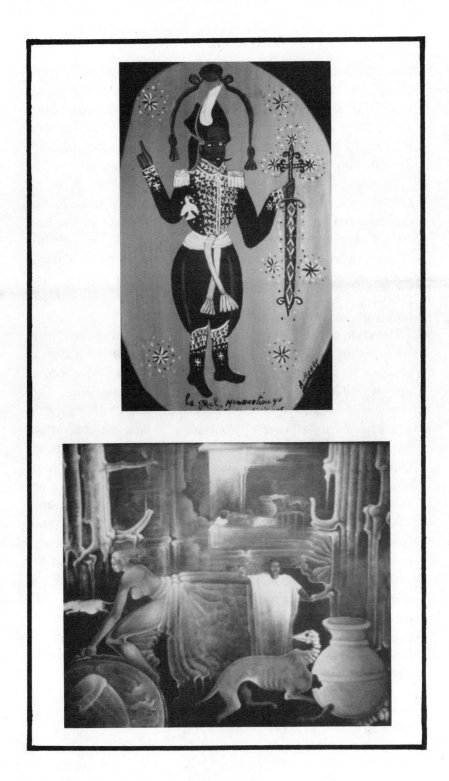

But the artist who had perhaps the most macabre imagination of all these artists was Edger Jean-Baptiste. His paintings were filled with terrific demons, *bocors, zombies,* with scenes set in cemeteries under a full moon. Unfortunately he never left his native Bainet until it was too late to treat the glaucoma that left him blind for life.

The label "surrealist" has been attached to all these artists, but the first to really merit it was Faustin. The monumental dreamscapes he painted shortly before his death in the later 1970's were invariably inspired by his *maît-tête, Erzulie Dantor,* who did not approve of his trips to New York in search of drugs. This jealous *loa* appears in Faustin's last great paintings, warning him of the death that finally came to him from an overdose[7] in Pétion-Ville.

The style of the Saint-Soleil masters, celebrating the *loas* in free-floating imagery but never depicting them in historical costume as Pierre, Vital, or Domond had done, was born in the late 1970's. Two Haitian intellectuals of the *élite,* Tiga Garoute and Maud Robart, conceived the idea of giving paints and brushes to a peasant "commune" whose nascent artists would have no knowledge of the commercialism already rampant in the capital's galleries and would therefore come up with "pure" styles of their own. It was a brilliant idea but unfortunately it fell prey to influences as impure as unforeseen.

André Malraux, the great French man of letters, anti-Fascist, and Gaullist Minister of Culture who had written so perceptively of the "primitive" art found in Africa and the South Pacific, made his first visit to Haiti in 1975 and was drawn as if by the figure of a *vaudun* goddess to the commune at Soissons la Montagne. His enthusiasm for the paintings of Louisiane St. Fleurant, Prospère Pierrelouis and Levoy Exil was understandable and admirable, but what he wrote in his posthumously published *L'Intemporel* was

---

[7]He most likely died from an overdose of heroin.

somewhat degraded by his patent unfamiliarity with the art of *vaudun.* He was unaware of inspired sculptors like Georges Liautaud and Nacius Joseph. Malraux's perception that the Saint-Soleil painters could (and did) paint the *loas* "out of costume" and in terms of their powers alone, was his principal contribution to the aesthetics of Haitian art, and an important one.

But it was about this time that the Saint-Soleil artists at Soissons forsook the "commune" in the belief that their "naiveté" was being exploited by Robart and Garoute.[8] And happily for the artists they found a patron as sympathetic and more understanding half-way down the mountain to Port-au-Prince. This was Roger Coster who, more than a decade before as manager of the Grand Hotel Oloffson, had promoted the art of a *vaudun* priest, Robert St. Brice, whose artistic style was as unorthodox as the Saint-Soleil group's. St. Brice's free-floating *loas,* in fact, had been seen by the Saint-Soleil artists in their commune and had given them a precedent for depicting the *loas* as "ideas" or "powers" rather than as "historical" characters. Their arrival at Coster's was therefore not only a "marriage made in heaven" but a God-given opportunity to sell their paintings without any compromise in content or style.

The work in the 1990's has been brought into full fruition by the painting of Louisiane St. Fleurant's two talented sons, Stivenson and Ramphis Magloire. Stivenson's ambitious work, like his brother's, is thoroughly grounded in *vaudun.* His *Guédés* and other demonic figures are never, like André Pierre's or Pauléus Vital's, depicted in revolutionary costumes or in specific *cérémonies,* but show instead the essence of the *loas.* Ramphis's darker, more mysterious paintings, with their haunting presences and weightless symbols seem to be more

---

[8]Their mentor Tiga told them that true artists do not create for money. Then they discovered that Tiga and Maude were selling their paintings abroad for very large sums.

abstract, but they too draw upon the *loas* with a night poetry that will be familiar to anyone who has ever visited a *tonelle* and seen the spirit of the African religion as it must have been in Africa and still is in Haiti—in the remoter parts of the country—and in the souls of its most imaginative artists.

Meanwhile a formidable artist having nothing to do with any group or gallery, Lafortune Félix, had brought the pure art of *vaudun* to an explosive height not seen since the days of Hyppolite. Félix, like Hyppolite, was a *houngan* from central Haiti, in his case from Pont Sondé, a village of the Artibonite river valley. His genius was discovered almost simultaneously and independently by Pierre Monosiet and myself.[9] Monosiet, who had started his career as DeWitt Peters' assistant at *Le Centre d'Art*, became in the 1970's the first director of the *Musée d'Art Haïtien*, and the first Haitian with an unerring taste for whatever was inventive and transcendental in Haitian art. He gave Lafortune canvases, brushes and paints, and nurtured his development at a time when his art could easily have been turned into kitsch in the hands of the commercial galleries.[10]

Lafortune's art at first was characterized by monumental figures of the *loas,* the *houngans* and the *mambos,* materializing with a brutal, almost frightening intensity. The figure of the *loa, Bossu Trois Cornes,* on the wall of his *houmfor* in Pont Sondé, which led to his discovery, was the prototypical image painted by him at this time. But Lafortune's feeling for color and form has transcended both Hyppolite's and André Pierre's. His conjuring up of classic myths, centaurs and

---

[9]I (Selden Rodman) discovered him through the murals on his *houmfor* in Pont Sondé, just as Monosiet did at the same time.

[10]After Monosiet's death in the early 1980's, his role as Lafortune's friend, protector and patron, was taken over by Carlos Jara, Chilean director of the Organization of American States (OAS) in Haiti. Lafortune today remains in Pont Sondé.

phoenixes—perhaps out of some depth of his subconscious—is unique in Haitian art.

Two other great Haitian sculptors besides the aforementioned Jasmin Joseph—Georges Liautaud in cut-out, forged metal, and Nacius Joseph in wood—were well established by the 1980's, and both were inspired by *vaudun*. Liautaud was discovered by DeWitt Peters and Jason Seeley when they happened to be passing through Croix-des-Bouquets on their way to the great salt lake on the Dominican border. As they were driving they noticed curiously embellished crosses on graves in the local cemetery. Asking around about who did these, they were directed to Liautaud's blacksmith shop. There they persuaded the artist to try his hand at free-standing figures in the cut-out iron which he handled as if he had been familiar with it all his life. Dusty Croix-des-Bouquets in the flat sugar-rich plain behind Port-au-Prince has always been a center of *vaudun* in Haiti. Liautaud was not a *houngan,* but he had been deeply affected by *vaudun* from his childhood on. Most of the sculptures which he began to hammer out in the 1960's and 1970's—some flat with cut-out patterns of flowers and figures, some free-standing with bracing supports—were inspired by *vaudun*.

Though many of his pieces early on were bought by the Museums of Modern Art in Paris and New York, and collectors world-wide were vying for the best, Liautaud would never leave Croix-des-Bouquets, which soon became renowned everywhere as the home of a dozen brilliant metal men. And his rare drawings (without perspective, bodies with crossing limbs whose junctures Liautaud disdained to erase, and often with both eyes to one side of the nose) have properly been compared to Picasso, an artist he never heard of and probably would not have understood.

Outstanding apprentices of Liautaud, like the late Murat Brièrre, Serge Jolimeau, Gabriel Bien-Aimé, the brothers Sérésier and Janvier Louisjuste, all of whom have never moved outside Croix-des-Bouquets, are as *vaudun* oriented as Liautaud. But unlike Liautaud all of them attach dangling elements to their larger pieces, and sometimes "engrave" the flat areas as if with a burin.

---

Facing page:

**Cross**
by Georges Liautaud.
Collection, Don Garrabrant, Chicago, Illinois

*Legba*
by Georges Liautaud.
Collection, Don Garrabrant, Chicago, Illinois

Facing page:

**Bossu Trois Cornes**
by Joseph Louisjuste.
Collection, Julia Hillman

**Simbi**
by Joseph Louisjuste.
Collection, Don Garrabrant, Chicago, Illinois

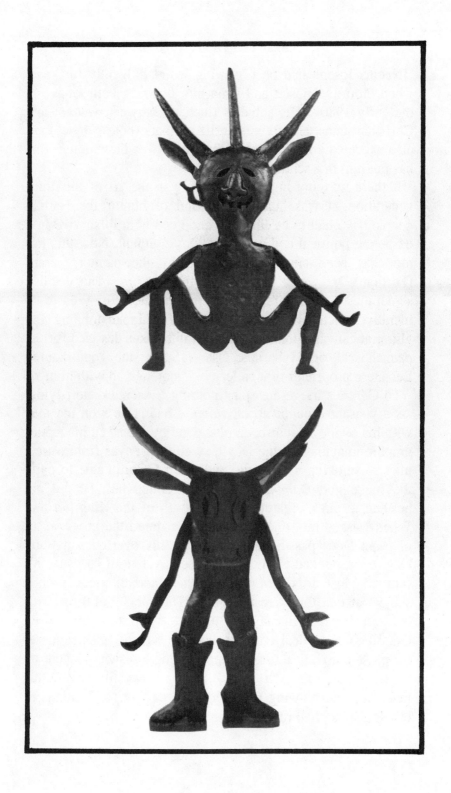

Nacius Joseph had been carving wood diligently for years when Pierre Monosiet and I ran him down in Petit Goave in the early 1980's. His subjects fluctuate between *vaudun* and Christian icons. His figures adrift in boats (boat people?) are also executed with passion and a feeling for the medium that has put him in a school by himself.

If there was any ingredient missing in the art of this third generation, it was humor—the kind of humor the Haitian people have had to be liberally endowed with to survive in a desperate political and ecological environment. Now this humor has been copiously supplied by the painter Gérard (Fortune). He was a pastry cook for the *élite,* who decided sometime in the 1970's, that it might be more fun (and more lucrative) to throw the equivalents of whipped topping and glitter at canvases than into indigestible cakes destined for the paunches of rich sybarites. Issa el Saieh, the good-natured Lebanese proprietor of a gallery in Pacot, agreed with him.

To Gérard's irreverent spirit nothing is sacred or terrifying. As a peasant brought up on *vaudun,* hadn't he seen the *loas* with his own eyes—or been possessed by them? In his iconographic imagination, the Devil, stealing papayas from a tree, may be smoking a cigarette, and when Gérard came to paint the snake god *Damballah* with his coiled tail, he did not hesitate to put a cigarette in the mouth of the King-*loa* too. When I asked him once why he had painted the gross poster of Papa Doc "passing the power" to his overfed son Baby Doc, he responded with the Créole equivalent of "because it's funny." Most artists would have hesitated to touch such a subject at that time because of the Duvaliers' political terror but not Gérard. It may be characteristic, too, that when Gérard came to deal with the Haitian War of Independence, he passed up all those pompous generals, who ended up feathering their nests, to instead paint a slave still wearing his manacles and blowing a conch shell; calling for Haitians to revolt against the French.

Gérard feels a strong kinship with animals. The ferocious dog with long teeth which figures in so many early pictures is also often carrying a basket of puppies. A picture of a thief on his back after trying to steal eggs from a nest is about to get what Gérard thinks he deserves—the loss of his tongue, plucked out by the furious mother bird. And Gérard has an ex-pastry chef's respect for food; in his painting, *Woman with Banana and Fish*, the woman is barely co-equal with the food.

Gérard also has what seems to be a fellow-feeling for athletes, perhaps because they too do what they do without talking about it. His *Brazilian Soccer Players* painted in 1983 was a worthy prelude to the great *Boxers* of the following year, in which the artist's archetypal memory seems to stretch back in time at least as far as Hector Hyppolite's (who used what seems to be Coptic-like iconography without ever having seen any Coptic art). Thanks to the observant eye of Dr. Edward Hehre, of the Albert Einstein College of Medicine, who had visited the volcanic Aegean island of Santorini off Crete and seen the Minoan fresco of two young boxers that dates back to 1550 B.C.E., the astonishing resemblance between the two works of art was seen. The stance of the Minoan youths, their profiled faces, the pear-shaped gloves and partial absence thereof, foreshadow Gérard's painting uncannily.

In his latest important pictures, Gérard reveals another resemblance that may be just as fortuitous. His figure of the two-faced, pipe smoking *marassas* wearing a Haitian revolutionary tricorn hat[11] recalls in its vatic gestures, fish-like appendages and restrained quasi-pointillist technique, the work of the Saint-Soleil masters.

Gérard's world is peopled with sexy *serviteurs* lighting candles and shaking *assons* while wearing red bikinis, with *arbres-reposoirs* where spirits seem to be organically part of

---

[11]This painting is now in the major German collection of Astrid and Halvor Jaeger.

their trees, with two-headed dogs and two-headed ladies, who depict the many moods of the *marassas.*

Carole has no doubts that *loas* visit Gérard in his mountain *caille* where he lives far above the bustle of Pétion-Ville. She has proof. In 1983 her ailing, eighty-one year-old mother died in our house in Jacmel, and although we had her body sent back to the United States for burial, Carole always felt her mother did not go with it. Several years later a friend, Joey Fabio, who is an art collector and old Haiti hand, visited our house in Jacmel during our absence and slept in Carole's mother's bed. Upon leaving he drove directly to Gérard's *caille* and discussed with him the possibility of buying several unfinished canvases. Making suggestions for minor changes, he arranged to come back the next day when the paintings would be ready. The pictures pleased him so much, he bought all of them although he noted that one had been altered drastically. When he had seen it the day before, it had been a clown, and now it was the portrait of a white woman in a print dress. On his return to the United States, Joey brought the paintings to show us in our house in New Jersey. When we saw them, we gasped. The changed painting was a perfect likeness of Carole's mother when she was young.

Several months later we visited Gérard and asked him about the picture.

"Was it someone you knew?" Carole asked.

He shook his head, no. This painting was especially strange for Gérard rarely painted white people.

"Then what inspired you to paint it?" Carole asked.

He thought for a minute.

"I don't know," he said, "she just came to me."

Overleaf:

**Portrait of Mrs. Earl Cleaver**
painted from life by Joseph Cummings Chase.
Collection, the Authors

**The Spirit Who Came To Me**
by Gérard, 1983.
Collection, Carole Cleaver, Oakland, New Jersey

## *Erzulie Dantor, Pètro* Goddess of Love

*Erzulie's Pètro* incarnations, *Erzulie Dantor* and *Erzulie ze Rouge*, are quite different from *Erzulie's Rada* forms. Their colors are red and black and their symbol is a heart into which a knife has been plunged. Jealous and angry, they demand complete control over their followers and the sacrifice of black pigs. When their *loas* are manifest in possession, tears come out in tantrums with bodies knotted and fists clenched.

# CHAPTER SIX

## *VAUDUN'S* DARKER SIDE: *BOCORS* AND BLACK MAGIC

A French con man with one ear had made his base in Jacmel for some years. When he decided he had squeezed the territory dry, he cut to Paris. But word of his plans to escape leaked out; and among those with debts to collect was a *bocor* (dealer in black magic) who promptly nailed the leg of a plastic doll pierced by a long, bloody needle to the con man's door. The Frenchman laughed good-naturedly, kept the evil *ouanga* (charm) as decor and flew home to Paris. Months later, while painting the ceiling of a restaurant he was redecorating, he fell from the ladder and received multiple fractures of the leg the *bocor* had cited for attention. Before he emerged from the hospital months later, limping with a cane, the news had traveled back to Jacmel by the Haitian *télediol* ("the grapevine"). People smiled, nodded their heads wisely and went about their business.

On the lighter side, the following story was related by Colonel Robert Debs Heinl, who headed the United States Marine military mission to Haiti in the early 1960's until he had had more of Papa Doc than he (or the Kennedy Administration) could take. Late in the 1960's, Heinl and his wife, who were living in Pacot, a suburb of Port-au-Prince, started writing the most completely documented history of Haiti in any language.[1] When he had finished a very critical chapter on the Duvaliers, Heinl had the typescript sealed in an envelope ready to mail to his publisher, Houghton Mifflin in Boston. But just as he was about to step into his car, a strange dog came out of nowhere and bit him in the leg. He dropped his manuscript to deal with the dog. The dog seized the package in its teeth and disappeared, never to be seen again. People said the dog was a *baka* (a demon in an animal's body) and Papa Doc, who was famous for dealing in black magic, had sent it to get rid of the offensive material.

Colonel Heinl had a carbon of the stolen manuscript, of course, and he was more careful next time, taking it home with him on the plane to Washington. Months later when it was being proof-read in the publisher's New York City office, the chapter on the Duvaliers again disappeared.

For two instances of effective black magic like these, there are no doubt hundreds of cases that had no consequences. But the failures are not reported. Who cares?

Alfred Métraux devotes an inordinate number of pages[2] to stories about people who profess to have been swindled by unscrupulous *bocors*. None of them are dramatic, and if they prove anything, they prove only that the raconteurs (*élites* for the most part) were eager to convince the "serious" French sociologist that they were above believing in such silly "peasant" superstitions. Tales of *zobops,* monsters conjured up by sorcerers and banded together in "red sects," *loup-garous* (werewolves) used to frighten recalcitrant children or naive journalists like William Seabrook in search of hot copy, owe as much, Métraux admits, to European treatises on black magic as to native imaginations.

---

[1] *Written in Blood: The Story of the Haitian People 1492-1971,* Robert Debs Heinl and Nancy Heinl, (Boston: Houghton Mifflin Co.), 1978.
[2] Forty-three in a book of moderate length.

Magic abounded in seventeenth and eighteenth century France. One of Louis XIV's mistresses, the Marquise de Montespan, is said to have consulted an infamous sorceress, La Voisin, to keep the Sun King's affections. This lady was later arrested for arranging black masses at which live children were sacrificed and naked court ladies served as altars.

Some of Métraux's stories involve *bocors* who play on the widely-held Haitian belief in treasure hoards of gold coin buried on their properties by French planters escaping the 1791 slave insurrection. The longest story is based on a transcript of the trial of a swindling magician which appeared in the newspaper *Le Nouvelliste* November 20, 1944. The victim, a Madame Tulia Durand, had paid thousands of dollars and numberless gems set in gold to a magician who convinced her that a treasure lay buried under her home. The wily *bocor* even showed Mme. Durand a genuine French coin or two. When the credulous lady finally lost patience and went to the police, the swindler was jailed for fraud—but too late for the lady to recover much of the loot.[3]

Our son, Van, during his teenage years chose to wear a silver *ankh*, the ancient Egyptian symbol of life, around his neck on a chain. A neighborhood friend in the southern town of Jacmel, where we then lived, assured him that the local *bocor* could cause this *ankh* to reproduce itself so that instead of one silver *ankh*, Van could have several.

One day Van showed the *ankh* to the *bocor*, who agreed to conduct the appropriate ceremony. Van was to select and buy three eggs in the local market and bring them together with a bottle of rum to our courtyard that evening. The *bocor* arrived as scheduled with several assistants, drew a *vever* on the stone floor, and set upon it several lighted candles and the three eggs. He began to chant and to drink rum and was soon possessed by *Baron Samedi*. The *loa* instructed Van to crush each

---

[3]Métraux, *op. cit.,* pp. 314-16.

egg between his hands. The first egg broke easily and contained nothing. The second egg refused to break although Van pressed with all his might. "This egg contains your strength," the *bocor* asserted, "you must eat all of it." Inside the third egg was a small *ankh*.

The *bocor* now demanded that the *loa* be rewarded for producing the new *ankh*. He instructed Van to give one of his assistants ten dollars which would be "thrown away" where the *loa* could find it. Van and the assistant went into the courtyard outhouse, and the assistant threw the ten dollar bill into the john. Peering down, Van saw that it had been propelled in such a way that it did not fall into the water but had stuck to the side where it could be easily retrieved.

The next morning Van ate the required egg. He then went to the outhouse to look for the money. It was gone. Encountering the *bocor* in the town square, Van proclaimed loudly that he had taken his ten dollars. Outraged, the *bocor* screamed that the *loa* would surely take vengeance on him.

That night the new *ankh* now on the chain about Van's neck burned an evil-looking spot on his chest. He was overcome by a fever so high he became delirious and nearly threw himself off our third floor balcony. "I deserve to die," he kept exclaiming, "I turned the world upside down." Tests taken at the hospital the next day indicated that Van did not have malaria or any other common disease found in tropical Haiti. Since there was no scientific explanation, they wracked their brains and decided it must be the much rarer *dengué fever*.[4]

In Chapter Two it was mentioned that all priests and priestesses of *vaudun* are familiar with black magic (*magie noire*)—they have to be to counter effectively the spells of unscrupulous *bocors*, themselves sometimes *houngans* who "serve with both hands." But the honest and worthy *houngan* will have nothing to do with practices designed to defraud the

---

[4]*Dengué fever* is a tropical disease, transmitted by an insect bite, characterized by swelling of the brain and a high fever.

innocent or put evil spells on a client's enemy. Of course if such a reputable *houngan* traps a sorcerer who turns out to be a thief or murderer, by turning his magic against him, the good *houngan's* flock (and the law) will applaud. The difference is in the priest's morality; and of that the *serviteur* must judge.

The *bocor* may work on his own, or in a *houmfor* devoted to the rites of *Pétro* where standards are lax. The grand master of sorcery is *Legba*—generally invoked in *Pétro* as *Maît-Carrefour*. Other disreputable *loas* invoked are *Criminelle*, a sinister aspect of *Ghédé*; *Erzulie Ze rouge; Ti-Jean;* and *Kitadémembre.*

Unlike the *houngans,* whose rites of *vaudun* are public and open to anyone, the *bocor* operates secretly, at the foot of black crosses in cemeteries or at lonely crossroads. Yet his "congregation," so to speak, is nation-wide. In a poor country like Haiti where literacy is confined to the upper and middle-classes, almost everyone has a basic knowledge of how to cast spells—and prepare poisons. Not that many would do any of these things, but to guard against them one must be prepared. And the best way to be prepared may be to know a magician.

Métraux tells the story of a friend of his, an anthropologist, who in her babyhood almost fell victim to a *bocor.* One day the victim's mother heard the child give a sharp cry followed by prolonged screams. The child's nurse could not account for it. Finally, since the screams continued, the mother took the child to her doctor who discovered a pin so deeply imbedded in the child's chest that he had to operate to take it out. The nurse was questioned a second time and now admitted that a *houngan* had told her that he must have an "angel before Christmas." The mother was too relieved to prosecute the nurse, but needless to say fired her.[5]

---

[5]Métraux, *op. cit.*, p. 271.

Maya Deren on the other hand—more personally involved in the cult since she lived with a *houngan* and describes her own possession—believed that the secrecy cloaking *magie noire* attests to its fundamental pessimism. As Haitians become less and less certain that the cosmos is essentially benevolent, they tend to turn away from the *Rada* rites and invoke the *bocor* who scorns the collective well-being in favor of his individualistic promises to "get things done." And since one of the functions of the *houngan* is to protect his people against the malevolent *ouanga* of the magician with protective *gardes* (talismans), he too must perform magic. "This has contributed," she writes, "to the great confusion between *Voudoun,* as a religious practice, and the magical practices, which are actually completely separate and outside the religious system. A man may be strong and powerful because the *loas* have made him so; but it is the man who makes the magic, not *loas.*[6]"

There are no "rites" in black magic. "A magician's apprenticeship consists of exchanging his services for secreted, concealed information, whereas the religious neophyte, by virtue of experience and ordeals, matures spiritually to an understanding of things which have been frankly evident in public ritual all along. Magic refers to power, which is amoral in nature; the primary emphasis of religion is moral discipline and development."[7] The *bocor,* Deren concludes, "is involved in a complex and formal series of cabbala-like manipulations, involving 'contacts,' publicity incantations, and even what might be accurately termed the cocktail libation...all pursued in the interests of his own personal aggrandizement and entirely irrespective, in a profound sense, of the public welfare."[8]

---

[6]Deren, *op. cit.*, p. 77fn.
[7]*Ibid.,* p. 200.
[8]*Ibid.,* p. 201.

If the credentials of Deren and Métraux be questioned because of their affiliations with the avant-garde in New York and Paris, no such case could ever have been made against the scholarly objectivity of Jean Price-Mars and Melville Herskovits. Price-Mars (1876-1969) was the father of Haitian ethnology and author of the 1928 classic *Ainsi Parla L'Oncle* which established once and for all the African provenance of *vaudun* as a religion and the dominant yet heretofore neglected component of Haitian culture. He was also the first of his countrymen to ridicule (albeit gently) the timorousness of the *élite* viz-a-viz all things African.

Price-Mars was the first to understand black magic, pointing out that magic from Moses[9] on down has been a component of all religions in their early stages. Melville Herskovits, for his part, disposed of the wholly undocumented canards of nineteenth and twentieth century sensationalists once accepted abroad at face value, that Haitians practice human sacrifice, cannibalism, and the wholesale creation of slaves by resuscitating the buried dead (*zombis*).

It was Salomon Reinach almost a century ago who pointed out that humanity, to justify such crimes as slavery and war, always "found an auxiliary in a false science which is the mother of all true science, Magic." And from there, Price-Mars goes on to point out that whereas *vaudun* concerns itself primarily with collective well-being through public rites, black magic reveals "a particularly individualistic character." Though "there are religious communities," he adds, "there are no magical communities."[10] In Dahomey, from which *vaudun* was introduced into St. Domingue by the preponderance of slaves the French colonists imported from that relatively enlightened kingdom in West Africa, sorcerers were hanged, stoned to death and left unburied.

---

[9]"I have given you blood," Jehovah tells him, "as a means of expiation for your souls at my altar." *Numbers,* XXVIII.
[10]Price-Mars, *op. cit.,* p. 42.

Rémy Bastien, an intelligent Haitian sociologist who has lived in Mexico for the last fifty years, reveres Price-Mars but believes that he tends to see peasant life as more idyllic than it is, ignoring the peasant's dependence on magic as a panacea in the struggle for survival.

Melville Herskovits, before addressing the relation of black magic to *vaudun* as no one else has, disposes of the various myths and misconceptions that have given Haiti a "bad press" for more than a century:

> More than any other single term, the word "voodoo" is called to mind wherever mention is made of Haiti...Not only has emphasis been placed on its frenzied rites and the cannibalism supposed on occasion to accompany them, but its dark mysteries of magic and "*zombies*" have been so stressed that it has become customary to think of the Haitians as living in an atmosphere of psychological terror...The system of belief included under the term *vodun* (and the rewards that accrue from practicing its rites in good faith) are good health, good harvests, and the goodwill of fellow-men; the punishment for neglect is corresponding ill fortune.[11]

So where does that leave black magic? And what is its relation to *vaudun*? And is the *houngan*, who seems to know so much about exorcising the *bocor's* spells—and even casting a spell or two himself if the occasion calls for it—a hypocrite?

No, answers Herskovits, but the distinctions are perforce subtle. Since the system of magic is empowered and validated by many of the *loas*, as well as being closely affiliated with the cult of the dead, "distinctions in practice are neither sharp nor consistent. Contradictions arise from the fact that the realistic African world view has by no means given way to that separation of the categories of good and evil that governs much of European thinking. A *loa* that helps a man when friendly to him may, if slighted or vexed, set about to do him harm. For the *loa*, like human beings, are creatures of mood

---

[11]Herskovits, *op. cit.*, pp. 139, 154.

and may take umbrage at some act which had created no displeasure before."[12] Moreover the *houngan* and the *bocor*, Herskovits points out, often employ essentially the same techniques and operate with the same forces, the differences between them being one of degree rather than of kind. "*Houngan*, c'est magazin. Gaigne enpil marchandise.—The *houngan* is like a shop. He has a lot of merchandise."[13]

Then what are the differences? "The gods of the *houngan*," Herskovits concludes, "are family gods who come to him through the natural course of inheritance, endowing him with the *connaissance* that gives him his control over the supernatural world, while the *bocor* buys his gods...a purchase dearly bought, bringing its own eventual punishment."[14]

Overleaf:
*La Grande Brigitte-La-Croix*
by André Pierre.
Private Collection

---

[12] *Ibid.*, pp. 222-23.
[13] *Ibid.*, p. 225.
[14] *Ibid.*

The following story was recounted to us by Tamara Baussan, a white Russian lady from Baku, who having fallen in love with a Haitian architectural student at the Ecole des Beaux Arts in Paris, married him, and moved to Haiti where she co-managed the Hotel Ibo Lélé for more than fifty years.

There was a large and beautiful tree in a Port-au-Prince cemetery, where, a *bocor* said, resided *Brigitte-la-Croix*, the wife of *Baron Samedi*. When the wind ruffled the branches, the faithful heard her voice and saw her floating among the foliage. Masses of people began to appear to leave gifts for her. Why? Because *La Grande Brigitte* was known to dispense money, and money is the primary need of every impoverished Haitian. Things began to get out of hand. The people trampled on neighboring graves and jostled each other, picking fights, while the offerings attracted various ravenous animals. Clearly something had to be done. The authorities built a high cement wall about the entire cemetery and attached to it strong metal gates, reinforced with a chain. The people were undaunted. They climbed the wall, slid under the gate, broke the chain. There was only one solution. In the dead of the night, the authorities sneaked into the cemetery and cut down the tree.

Facing page:

*An Avan, An Avan!* **(Forward, Forward!)**
by Hector Hyppolite, c. 1947.
*Zombis* being returned to the grave by a *bocor* (sorcerer).
Collection, Musée d'Art Haïtien, Port-au-Prince, Haiti

**Creation of a *Zombie***
by Lafortune Félix, 1984.
Collection, Charles Boer, Pomfret, Connecticut

# *Baron Samedi,* God of Death

*Baron Samedi,* is the chief of the *Guédés,* the spirits who inhabit the cemetery and the underworld. He wears a top hat, sunglasses, and smokes a cigar. His color is black, and he prefers as a sacrifice, a black goat. His symbol is the cross. Those possessed by him make obscene gestures and demand food, rum and tobacco. A glutton and a trickster, he is also worshipped as *Baron-La-Croix* and *Baron Cimitière.* His wife, *Brigitte-La-Croix,* or *Grande Brigitte,* is the evil goddess of black magic and ill-gotten gold. Always dressed in purple, she lives in the trees of cemeteries and prefers the sacrifice of black chickens.

# CHAPTER SEVEN

## *VAUDUN* IN HAITIAN HISTORY

One sometimes wonders whether the peaceful serenity in which most Haitian peasants live, and the inevitable reflection of that serenity in their arts, is an antidote to the incredible violence found in the more than two centuries of Haitian history. The well-documented atrocities which the French masters visited upon their slaves, and the similar horrors perpetrated in retaliation by the ex-slaves in 1791—and after 1803 upon each other, blacks against mulattoes, mulattoes against blacks, a racist counterpoint of violence unceasing to this day—is not apparent to the casual visitor.

It surfaced, as already noted in these pages, at the *vaudun* ceremony of 11 August 1791 in an alligator swamp on the outskirts of Cap Haïtian called Bois Caïman. It was there that the *papaloi,* Boukman, gave final orders to the other leaders of the conspiracy for the attack on the great plantation houses a week later. Pillage, arson, rape and murder followed inevitably. It was not that *vaudun* (even in the *Pètro* form practiced at Bois Caïman) is violent in itself, but that the then sacred African religion (as St. Méry had warned in his great study of a debased colony about to commit suicide) was ideally available to mask subversion. Participants in Boukman's fateful conclave, if the French had questioned them,[1] would have resorted to the stock answer: *vaudun* as all could see, was good clean fun.

The totalitarian military dictators who were Haiti's first successful leaders knew better. Toussaint Louverture, the mildest of them, outlawed the cult during his brief rule (1798-1802). Before Napoleon's veteran division captured him and deported him to his death in an Alpine prison,[2] Toussaint had understood that the colony's unprecedented wealth in coffee, cotton, sugar and indigo could never be restored in devastated

---

[1] Had a rebellious slave been put to the torture—touching off gunpowder in the bodies' orifices and burial alive were favorite French methods—he would not have likely revealed *vaudun's* secrets. After all, had not the revered *papaloi* promised eternal delights in the African hereafter to any slave harmed by the hated masters?

[2] Toussaint in 1802 was directing the second phase of the ex-slaves' resistance to Napoleon's effort to retake what had been France's richest overseas possession, when the French commander, General Leclerc, Bonaparte's brother-in-law, made his move—on orders from Paris, of course, but with the urgency of the epidemic of Yellow Fever that was threatening to decimate his troops. The "second phase" was guerrilla warfare which Toussaint was directing from his estate at Ennery. Two French frigates, just arrived off Gonaïves, had already begun to land men. The black leader, a few miles inland, had already been warned of his peril, but he agreed to meet Brunet, one of Leclerc's officers. The two were parleying amicably when Brunet left the room and the French marines seized Toussaint, took him aboard a frigate, and then transferred him to a larger ship, the *Héros,* whence he was taken to France. From Brest, on July 2nd, he was transferred overland to the Fort de Joux in the Juras on the border of Switzerland. There, in a cell twenty feet long by twelve feet wide, shivering and shaking, poorly clad, and barely given enough food to stay alive, he survived until the mountains were covered with snow. On Napoleon's orders one jailer succeeded another, until the last one gave orders that his one luxury, coffee, be withdrawn. On April 7, 1803, Toussaint was found dead in his chair. Eleven years after his death, Napoleon, facing his own end on St. Helena admitted that he had made a great mistake to send the ill-fated Leclerc and his army to St. Domingue. "I should have been content to accept the offer of Toussaint Louverture to govern the colony through him."

St. Domingue except by labor—and that, from ex-slaves who had tasted freedom, meant forced labor.

Toussaint was ruthless but intelligent. His principal lieutenant, Jean-Jacques Dessalines, who took over after the French had finally been driven out in 1803, was more ruthless and ferociously racist viz-a-viz the mulattos as well as the whites, but stupid. Not stupid enough, however, to ignore the fact that *vaudun* ceremonies would be just as dangerous to overseers wielding native liannes (vine ropes) as it had been to French field bosses with their whips. Once Dessalines had crowned himself Emperor without distributing lesser honoraria to his cronies (*"Moi seul je suis noble!"* he had said) his brief reign was doomed. His mulatto successor in Port-au-Prince, Alexandre Pétion, was not a *vaudouist*,[3] but he was intelligent enough to know that he could not survive if the *houngan*s turned against him. He and his mulatto successors, therefore, tolerated the religion, and even cemented the alliance by giving the *houngan*s liberal grants of land.

In the North, all the way from Gonaïves to Ouanaminthe on the Dominican border, another of Toussaint's commanders, Henry Christophe, held sway. Pétion left him alone after failing to defeat him in battle. English-born on the island of St. Christopher (St. Kitts)—hence his two names—Christophe soon crowned himself King Henry I and built the palace Sans Souci and the immense fortress of La Citadelle Laferrière, for which he is famous. But like Toussaint and Dessalines, he wanted no truck with *vaudun*. His excuse for proscribing its practice, like Toussaint's, was that he was a good Catholic. Yet the totalitarian methods he employed to get the palace of Sans Souci and the mountain-top fortress La Citadelle built were just as draconian as the other two military chieftains', and finally resulted in his regime's overthrow at his death.

---

[3]He had been educated in France along with other light-skinned *affranchis.*

With Haiti united again and sinking into the economic slump that still plagues it, laissez-faire continued for *vaudun* as well until Faustin Soulouque, a black as ruthless as Dessalines, took over in 1846. He crowned himself Emperor Faustin I six years later and set up a full complement of titled nobility. Faustin Soulouque was a practicing *vaudouist* himself, and during his reign *cérémonies* took place in the palace with the ruler and his wife officiating as *houngan* and *mambo*.

It was under Emperor Faustin's reign, with the French-oriented mulatto *élite* thoroughly cowed by firing squads and deportations, that *vaudun* became so entrenched it could never be eradicated by force. Faustin had no use for the Catholic priests, and during his tenure, which lasted until 1859, Rome fared badly. When Pope Pius IX refused to supply an Archbishop to officiate at the coronation, Faustin found a renegade "bishop," Abbé Cessens, curé of Port-au-Prince, who was happy to anoint the crown with holy oil to the strains of the Episcopal "Veni Creator Spiritus."[4]

When Faustin Soulouque finally abdicated after his third futile attempt to occupy Spanish Santo Domingo, the palace was taken over by the ablest and most benign of his officers. Next on Soulouque's list for execution, Fabre Geffrard took the oath of office on January 18, 1859, declared the Empire dead, and reinstated the Constitution of 1846. In 1860 a Concordat between the Vatican and Haiti was signed, and two years later the United States, during the Civil War, recognized Haiti along with Liberia. But on December 31 of that year, President Lincoln signed a contract engaging the American government to pay one Bernard Kock two hundred and fifty thousand dollars for settling five thousand freedmen at Ile-à-

---

[4]Père Cabon, Haiti's priestly historian, reveals that Cessens, far from having been consecrated archbishop or given the holy oil by Pius, as he claimed, actually skipped Rome after being ordered by the Pope into arrest in a nearby monastery. As for the holy oil, Cabon sniffed, it was ordinary Marseilles olive oil. For the full story of Faustin's put-down of the Catholic Church, see the Heinls' *Written in Blood*.

Vache, a small satellite in the harbor of Les Cayes. The contract was signed against the advice of the Attorney General who for over a month had been denouncing Kock as a fraud.[5] Lincoln realized his mistake in time to rescind the order, but Kock actually managed to collect several hundred deluded ex-slaves, take ship, and land them on the then-uninhabited islet where most of them perished of thirst.

What was Fabre Geffrard's attitude toward *vaudun*? Fortunate to be neither black nor mulatto—he was what the Haitians call a *griffe*, which is three quarters black and one quarter white—Geffrard was for all that an *élite* Catholic, and he had no use for the cult that had sustained the Emperor. The celebrated Affaire de Bizoton—a canard charging a *houngan* with child-sacrifice and cannibalism circulated by the racist British consul, Sir Spenser St. John—gave Geffrard his chance to crack down on *vaudun* as no President had done since the Haitian Revolution. Supported by the powerful Masonic Lodges, and of course by all the Christian churches, Geffrard survived for eight very turbulent years. He made many progressive reforms, but like most Haitian rulers, he reacted to opposition by becoming more and more repressive. Acquiring a personal fortune, he attempted to solve economic problems by printing paper money.

Geffrard's principal rebel opponent, Sylvain Salnave, lost battle after battle in trying to overthrow the President but never gave up. When he finally forced Geffrard to flee to Jamaica, he entered Port-au-Prince wearing the uniform of a Dominican carabinero—a Panama sombrero, a blue serape and jackboots; he flourished a huge machete as flowers rained down on him. His first action was to declare the British consul, Sir Spenser St. John, *persona non grata* because of his open hostility to *vaudun*. St. John retaliated by calling the new President's *vaudun* connections notorious—which they

---

[5]According to Ludwell Lee Montague, who relates this incident in his *Haiti and the United States: 1714-1938.*

were. Salnave resented the Concordat with Rome and his
most trusted advisor, Jean-Pierre Ibo, was a *houngan*.

Salnave was an honest man, with no taste for money. Worse
still, commented Frédéric Marcelin, the *élite's* snobbish
scribe, "O shame, women, compromised by debauch, haunt
every corner of the palace!" Milking the treasury for defen-
sive armaments, three thousand Salnavian *gourdes* were soon
worth only one dollar. He made enemies in every part of the
country until finally, victim of a tri-partite civil war, Salnave
was shot by a firing squad in the ruins of the palace his foes
had already blown up.

During the remainder of the nineteenth century and on into
the twentieth, *vaudun* was alive and well, so subtly syncretized and melded with Roman Catholicism that the priests and
bishops—mostly Breton *blancs* by this time—were hard put
to distinguish one cult from the other. When one of the *loas*
appeared at a public ceremony, Catholic prayers and devo-
tions predominated; and chromo-lithographs of the Virgin
Mary and Saints adorned every *houmfor* altar. Who was to
say that every *serviteur* recognized *Erzulie* in Mary, *Damballah* in St. Patrick with his serpent, *Ogoun* the warlord in
St. George with his flaming sword? If the village curé understood the connections, he kept his peace.

When Antoine Simon succeeded Pierre Nord-Alexis as
President in 1908, H.W. Furniss, the American Minister, sent
home this report:

> The President and his family are full of superstitions and are
> devotees of the *voudeaux* (sic). This devotion is of long standing
> and while he was still Military Governor in the South, he went
> so far as to have a mass said by the Bishop of Aux Cayes over a
> white goat which for a long time had figured as an emblem of
> the President's faith. The goat died and was brought with great
> pomp and ceremony to the cathedral in a closed coffin, and the
> Bishop, at the request of "Délégué Simon," not suspecting that
> the coffin contained a goat, said the mass. Later the Bishop
> found out what had been done and issued an order that in future

funeral masses the corpse must be exposed to the priest just prior
thereto...[6]

It was this same Furniss who, when asking Simon's new Fi-
nance Minister why Wall Street was not included in the itin-
erary of a special commission leaving for France to solicit a
loan, was told by the Minister with a laugh that the trip was
nothing but "a pleasure jaunt at the government's expense,"
and that on their twelve thousand dollar allowances the members would prefer to "spend their time in Paris on the Boule-
vards, at the Moulin Rouge, and like places dear to most Haitians."[7]

Writing of Simon's successor, Cincinnatus Leconte, a puppet of Imperial Germany, Joseph Pyke, the British Minister,
noted that the new President was cracking down on *vaudun*,
describing it as a *culte grossier*. There was no doubt, Pyke's
report to London added, "of the general practice of *Vaudoux*
among the peasants. I have myself seen within a half a mile of
Port-au-Prince a place of worship—temple, sacred tree, sacrificial stone and graves—with all the paraphernalia of dag-
gers, skulls, pots of blood and feathers and a priest in daily
attendance."[8]

Unfortunately there was no Joseph Campbell in England at
that time to remind Her Majesty's snob of Christian
"paraphernalia" and its murderous repressions. *Vaudun* was
indeed alive and well, but its reputation abroad—then as
now—was in the hands and mouths of Christian sensation-
mongers.

Under the Occupation of Haiti by American Marines—trig-
gered by the anarchy in Port-au-Prince which culminated in
the lynching of the bloodstained President Guillaume Ville-

---

[6]Heinl, *op. cit.*, p. 347.

[7]*Ibid.*, p. 349. If Furniss had ever heard of similar "official" joyrides by
United States Senators, paid for as liberally by that august body, he gave
no indication of it.

[8]*Ibid., p. 363.*

brun Sam at the French Embassy on July 28, 1915—*vaudun* took center stage infrequently. In 1918, wearing the scarlet badge of *Ogoun,* Charlemagne Peralte, commander of five thousand Cacos[9] almost captured Hinche, Charlemagne's hometown in central Haiti. Charlemagne's sister, a *mambo,* held a *nouvene* (novena) intended to "paralyze and confuse" the Gendarmerie guarding the capital. When they attempted to storm Port-au-Prince, Charlemagne's "divisions" (three hundred men) were easily repulsed, and shortly thereafter the flamboyant guerrilla leader himself was ambushed by U.S. Marine Sergeant H. H. Hanneken (who had been breveted into a Captain in the Occupation's *Gendarmerie*) near Grande Rivière on October 30, 1919.[10] The fact that Peralte's dead body was tied to a door so that it could be photographed for positive identification, led to the legend that he had been "crucified"—though in the famous paintings of that event by Philomé Obin some thirty years later, Charlemagne's body is properly tied.

Under the last of the mulatto puppet presidents the U.S. Marines had installed in the Palace, Élie Lescot, a concerted campaign was launched to stamp out *vaudun.* During the summer of 1941 *houmfors* all over Haiti were raided, sacred Mapou trees were cut down, drums and other equipment of the cult were burned. The campaign was strongly supported by *vaudun's* old enemies, the mulatto *élite* and the Roman Catholic Church; and by the French who told John Campbell White, soon to be named Washington's first Ambassador to Haiti, such obvious lies as that the *houngans* were "Vichy-oriented" and "pro-Nazi."[11]

Lescot's campaign had no long-range effect on *vaudun.* Nor did President Roosevelt's absurd wartime program to produce

---

[9]Cacos were peasant guerillas who had been active in Haiti for generations.
[10]Heinl, *op. cit.,* pp. 456-59.
[11]*Ibid.,* p. 538.

rubber from cryptostegia, a weed that abounded in the South, which only resulted in the laying-waste of one hundred thousand acres (five percent of Haiti's best land) with exactly five tons of rubber to show for it when the project was abandoned. *Houmfors*, needless to say, were bulldozed into oblivion along with the fruit trees of the forty thousand families shoveled off their lands for temporary employment.

In 1946 Lescot fled to Canada and was replaced by Dumarsais Estimé, a left-wing black teacher from the Artibonite river valley, who was supported by a Communist popularfront, but more importantly by a triumvirate of black officers who controlled the Armed Forces, and by liberals in the United States who had launched a vociferous campaign which had induced Roosevelt to lift the Marine Occupation in 1934. Soon the *vaudun*-inspired arts began to flourish with worldwide renown, and in 1946 Estimé's Minister of Education outraged the Catholic Church and the *élite* by presiding over a *fête* in the Ciné Rex, the only theater and movie house in Port-au-Prince, that featured *vaudun* chants and dances. When the Catholic newspaper, *Action Sociale*, called for a new campaign against the *houmfors*, the government's police suppressed the newspaper and jailed its editor. A French priest who had charged involvement in politics by the *houngans* was expelled from Haiti.

*Vaudun* came into its own, as it had not since the reign of Soulouque, when Dr. François Duvalier, himself a *vaudouist* and possibly a *houngan*, was elected to the presidency in 1957. But by the same token the cult suffered its most serious disfigurement. Could it ever recover from the association of so many of its priesthood in the grisly politics of "Papa Doc?"

Once Duvalier had thrown off his mask as a quiet country doctor-ethnologist—which had fooled everyone, including the American Embassy and the Episcopal Church which had supported his candidacy—it was too late. Not only was Duvalier determined to peel off Haiti's French veneer, replace white Breton priests with black Haitian ones, and break the long ascendancy of the mulatto business class; he permitted his identification in the public mind with *Baron Samedi* to be confirmed. Many, in fact, were certain now that "Papa Doc" must be a *bocor*—a certainty reinforced by his well-known obsession with astrology and numerology.[12]

When the "new Papa Doc" had disposed of Clément Jumelle, the last of his opponents in the 1957 election—Déjoie and Fignolé, his other two opponents in the election, had already been forced into exile—Jumelle's body was snatched from its coffin on the way from Sacré Coeur to the cemetery by *Tonton Macoutes,* the President's already ubiquitous secret police, and buried with *vaudun* rites in St. Marc. It was the unprincipled *Macoutes*, with their black glasses and bulging sidearms, who tarnished the reputation of the African cult. Venal *houngans*, grateful for *vaudun's* support in the palace, had not hesitated to join the *Voluntaires de la Securité Nationale* as the pistol-packing secret police came to be known officially.

The fact that Duvalier did not entirely trust these cult allies was demonstrated one evening in 1959 when truckloads of soldiers deployed in the dark, surrounded the major *houmfors* in Croix-des-Missions and Croix-des-Bouquets, *vaudun's* heartland. *Houngans* and *mambos* were seized unceremoniously and driven to the Palace, where, according to Rémy Bastien who first told the story,[13] they were taken to confront the President in his blood-red robe of the *Secte Rouge*, a *Pétro* society of sorcerers. "Never forget," President Duvalier was reported to have told them, "I am your master." Then he dismissed them—frightened into submission, Bastien says.

One other reported appearance of "Papa Doc" in his *Secte Rouge* costume is said to have occurred in August of 1962. President Kennedy had landed a Marine battalion in full battle

---

[12]The magical number 22, for example, figured in the timing of many Duvalierist political decisions.

[13]*Vodun and Politics in Haiti,* Rémy Bastien, (Washington, D.C., 1966).

gear at Bizoton in response to Paul Blanchet's huzzahs for Khruschev and Castro in his Communist-line (and of course Duvalierist) *Panorame*. Frightened, "Papa Doc" had his bags packed and was ready to flee to the Colombian Embassy, when the order was prematurely issued to the Marines to withdraw. On November 22—a selection of dates that Haitians noted—"Papa Doc" presided over a *cérémonie* in Bois Caïman in honor of the original *Pétro* insurrection against the French. At the ceremony in the Palace, *ouangas-à-mort* were issued for President Kennedy and his Marine commander. When Kennedy was assassinated in Dallas on 22 November, 1963, Haitians duly recalled "Papa Doc's" magic date. And when President Johnson, repudiating the Kennedy *démarche* against Duvalierism, resumed full American aid to Haiti, and sent Nelson Rockefeller to publicly embrace the tottering *bocor* on the Palace balcony, it seemed that sorcery had triumphed.

The fact that it had not was demonstrated on January 6, 1978 when a *bocor* in Gonaïves had a bull buried alive with a photograph of another American president, Jimmy Carter (who connected aid to respect for human rights), dangling from its neck. The American President survived the fateful date this time, and the Carter pressure for resumption of human rights was resumed.

When François Duvalier died in his bed on April 21, 1971, the Haitian Cassandras who were "Papa Doc's" enemies were well aware that the dread date was upon them. On the 22nd a strong wind blew, raising so much dust that the air was opaque, and it was difficult to see. His anointed son and successor, "Baby Doc" Duvalier, who stood in candlelight in the Palace as the *maît-tête* was transferred to him from his father, was surely aware of the cosmic occurrence. On April 24, the day of *Baron Samedi,* François Duvalier was buried.

It was not until "Baby Doc" fled the country, sixteen years later, that the mobs had sufficient courage to storm the Duvalier crypt. They tore it open with machetes, determined to mutilate and burn the hated dictator's body and by that action ensure the death of his soul. But their efforts were not rewarded. The tomb was empty.

Under the sixteen-year reign (1971-1986) of Jean-Claude Duvalier that followed, political tensions relaxed, tourists returned in record numbers, and the benign *Rada* face of *vaudun* was visible as never before. The iron fist beneath the velvet glove was still present in the Palace, however, descending mercilessly on political conspirators and would-be ones. But to the casual visitor things were quiet and travel within the country was unrestricted. Under Max Beauvoir, a suave *houngan* who had lived abroad and spoke English, Spanish and Portuguese as well as French and Créole, a nightclub, Le Peristyle de Mariani, was opened at which ceremonies were staged so realistically that susceptible guests as well as *hounsis* sometimes went into trance inadvertently.

The extent to which venal *houngans* were recruited by the *Tonton Macoutes*, as they had been under "Baby Doc's" father, is hard to determine; but the widespread perception that they were became apparent shortly after Jean-Claude and his acquisitive wife, Michèle Bennett, were forced to quit the country on February 7, 1986 with most of Haiti's moveable wealth in their pockets or Swiss bank accounts.

In May of that year, while the armed forces of the "caretaker" dictator, General Henri Namphy, stood by, bands of Catholic and Protestant fanatics ran wild all over Haiti for three days, burning *houmfors* to the ground, destroying drums and other sacred objects, and (especially in the south peninsula where *vaudun* has always been strongest) murdering *houngans* and other unarmed *serviteurs* who had had the hardihood to resist. Beauvoir and his flock in Mariani survived only because they were protected by iron doors and a six-foot wall over which flaming oil was hurled down on the rampaging attackers.

Like the last such official attack on *vaudun* under Lescot almost fifty years before, this one failed to accomplish its mission. *Vaudun* in Haiti remains as popular as ever, weakened only to the extent that during the Duvalierist terror the enforced complicity of the weaker *houngans* emboldened Christian enemies, especially those abroad, to depict *vaudun* in the most sinister hues.

*Serviteurs*, however, had reason to be nervous, when the new President, elected by the people on December 16, 1990, was a former Catholic priest. Père Jean-Bertrand Aristide, nonetheless, promised to rule with the guidance of two documents, the *Bible* and the Haitian Constitution. The latter, overwhelmingly endorsed by the people in 1987, states that all religions shall have the right to operate freely.

Aristide was deposed by the military in September, 1991, and while the new regime violently attacked his supporters, it left the *houngans* alone.

Facing page:

**La Sirène Fishing**
by Rigaud Benoit, 1986.
Collection, Don Garrabrant, Chicago, Illinois

*La Sirène*
by Serge Jolimeau, 1985.
Collection, Charles Boer, Pomfret, Connecticut

# *Legba,* Guardian of the Crossroads

*Legba* stands at the apex of the cross, where the spiritual and material worlds intersect. He is the first *loa* called at every ceremony for only he can open the gates and allow the spirits to descend. A very old man, *Legba* is pictured as a cripple and always carries a cane. His sign is the cross and his color black. A *macoute* (straw sack) which hangs from a tree sacred to him on the *houmfor* grounds, is kept filled with food.

# CHAPTER EIGHT

## *VAUDUN* VARIATIONS IN OTHER LANDS

African slaves were brought to many other parts of the Western Hemisphere besides Haiti, of course, and they brought their native spirits with them. But nowhere else, save in Brazil, did *vaudun* in the broader sense ever really flourish. *Santería* in Puerto Rico, *shango* in Cuba, Jamaica and Dutch Guiana, took recognizable forms and still persist vestigially. But perhaps because the cult of *Arada* (*Rada*) had become the state religion in the kingdom of Dahomey, from which the majority of slaves in St. Domingue came, *vaudun* in Haiti caught on as nowhere else; and because conditions in Haiti, as we have seen, contributed to its isolation from other cults at crucial times, it became the state religion, unchallenged, pervasive, ineradicable. With the diaspora of hundreds of thousands of poor Haitians to Miami and New York, *vaudun* migrated with them.

### BRAZIL: THE BACKGROUND

To understand why *umbanda*, *macumba*, *batuque*, and above all *condomblé* in the predominantly black state of Bahia, are African-derived cults flourishing in Brazil, a bit of Brazilian history, especially that part involving the unique relation of black slaves to white masters, may be helpful.

"If I were asked to name the one point in which there is a complete difference between the Brazilians and ourselves," wrote Theodore Roosevelt after his visit to Brazil in 1913, "I should say it was the attitude toward the black man."

In Brazil the terms *branco* (a white) and *preto* (a black) are used mainly to describe differences in physical appearance. *Preto* can describe a person with noticeably Negroid features, or a person of low social status, or even sometimes a personal enemy, but never does it connote racial inferiority (as did the word Negro in the United States until quite recently). As in Haiti, there is a saying among those of African descent, "A rich man is a white, but a poor white is black." Another Bahian saying goes, "The more money you have, the whiter you are." In the 1940's Donald Pierson, a black American sociologist, wrote: "Discrimination involving colored people often exists, but there is no racial discrimination. Color in Brazil is one of the criteria of rank."

Years ago in Brazil there were social, tennis and racing clubs in which no black had achieved membership. Until recently, the officer corps of the Navy was entirely white, and blacks are only now advancing beyond the non-commissioned ranks of the Army and Air Force. But foreigners will be wrong if they conclude from such evidence that a color bar exists. The fact is that very few Brazilians of African descent have thus far had the wherewithal (and therefore the higher education) to move up in such institutions of the socially élite. The few hotels which still refused accommodations to blacks in the 1970s did so because they were catering (or thought they were catering) to the imported prejudices of their guests. Writing in the time of slavery itself, Sir Richard Francis Burton remarked, "Nowhere, even in oriental countries has the 'bitter draught' so little gall in it."

Although the first African slaves were imported to Brazil as early as 1531, and in considerable numbers by 1550, Amerindian slaves performed most of the manual labor in the colony until 1600. In that year Brazil's population of one hundred thousand (excluding Amerindians) comprised thirty thousand Europeans, twenty-five thousand Africans, and forty-five thousand persons of mixed descent. A century later the balance had shifted drastically: one million five hundred thousand slaves of African descent outnumbered white colonists by more than two to one. The first complete census, taken in 1798, revealed 1,010,000 whites, 250,000 "civilized Amerindians," 406,000 freedmen, 221,000 mulatto slaves, and 1,361,000 black slaves—slaves in the total population of 3,248,000 again outnumbering the total of other groups by more than two to one. The few who bothered to defend slavery did so on two grounds: 1) that God had created the African as a "natural slave;" and 2) that his conversion from "barbarism" to Christianity more than compensated for the loss of freedom.

Long before the belated emancipation of the Brazilian slaves in 1888 by the Emperor Dom Pedro II's daughter, Princess Isabel, the African-Brazilians exhibited characteristics that distinguished them from most blacks imported into white colonies. They had acquired these characteristics because, for one thing, the Portuguese themselves had learned to co-exist with other races, including the Moors from 711 to 1244. There is a story that when an earlier Portuguese King, Manoel, wanted to marry a Spanish princess, and agreed to the condition that he must first purge his kingdom of all Jews, his chief minister, bringing in the decree of expulsion for him to sign, said: "Which of us shall leave, Sire, you or me?" The Moors no doubt reminded the Portuguese of Mohammed's preaching: "A man who ill-treats his slaves will not enter Paradise." Many of the slaves in both Portugal and Brazil came from Muslim countries, bringing with them a culture and education superior to those of their masters.

Against the indignities and cruelties of slavery, the slaves defended themselves as best they could. *Capoeira*, a technique for disarming an attacker with acrobatic footwork, was not always a dance. It was in part because the propaganda of the Abolitionists was beginning to cause restlessness among the slaves that the 1888 emancipation was proclaimed ahead of schedule.

Nevertheless much credit belongs to the Portuguese for not engendering a spirit of racial hostility among the blacks. Many slaves were freed unconditionally by their masters. Domestic slaves were treated especially well. Mulatto mistresses were considered more desirable than white ones. The famous Chica da Silva in Diamantina reproached her lover for not taking her aboard ship to Portugal, whereupon he built her a ship on which she could recline in her brocades, and floated it on an artificial lake. The poets, notably Castro Alves of Salvador, sang the praises of African Brazilians and denounced their subjugation. The Royal Family of Brazil in Petrópolis set an example by treating talented blacks as equals. Most important, perhaps, children of mixed unions tended to be drawn into the dominant culture, not made outcasts as they were in the United States.

Following emancipation, the freed blacks enjoyed no benefits—economic, social or political. Nor did they feel that Brazil had any special responsibilities towards them other than as citizens. They knew that whatever they achieved would be up to them. This lack of rancor, so bewildering to militants from abroad, persists to this day. Brazilians of African descent, regardless of their skin color and the pride they take in their African cultural heritage, consider themselves Brazilians. Some, like Aleijadinho, the great baroque sculptor, and Machado de Assis, Brazil's foremost novelist, seem to have taken little or no interest in their African ancestry. But today there is a growing appreciation of that heritage, and in particular of the transplanted African religions that are beginning to fertilize the arts as well as the lives of those who participate in them.

## CANDOMBLÉ

Oldest and purest of the tribal cults in Brazil is *candomblé*. It is practiced most frequently in Bahia, though its influence is beginning to spread as far south as São Paulo. Only in *candomblé* are the ties with Africa nurtured—and even renewed through visits and the importation of cult objects like raffia and cowry shells. *Candomblé* is a conservative religion. Not only do *candomblé's* devotees place great stress on the *orixás'* African names and identities, preserving the Nagô-Yoruba words in their incantations, but they also tend to be group-oriented and not political. They rarely if ever go into trance spontaneously, and they place the cult's major emphases on ritual and divination, initiation and sacrifice.

Who are the deities of *candomblé*? How are they worshipped? And for what reasons?

Corresponding to Christianity's all-powerful "God" is *Olorún,* significantly not worshipped at all either in West Africa or in Brazil because he is considered too mighty to be concerned with the trials and trivia of mere mortals. *Oxalá*[1] is the most exalted member of the Yoruba pantheon. Son of *Olorún,* he is father of the other gods, sovereign healer, spirit of procreation, bi-sexual. Other important deities in *condomblé* are *Iemanjá* (Our Lady of Conception), the sea-goddess now represented as a mermaid; *Omolú* (Saint Lazarus), fearsome master of plagues, diseases and death, who may not be looked in the face and who therefore "appears" at rites masked; *Xangô* (Saint Jerome), Thor-like god of thunder and fire, especially popular in Rio de Jañiero and Recife; *Iansa* (Saint Barbara), *Xangô's* wife, who dances aggressively, brandishing a copper scimitar; *Oxossi*, the hunter who carries a bow; *Ogoun*, divine blacksmith, god of war, patron of handicrafts and industry; and *Exú*, incorrectly identified with the devil but derived from the West African *Legba*, messenger of the

---

[1]Corresponding in Bahia to the city of Salvador's most important sub-deity, Our Lord of Bonfim, the crucified Christ.

gods. *Exú,* a trickster who must be placated before the other gods are invoked, haunts the crossroads; he is venal, facetious, phallic, violent, not to be trifled with.

As in Haitian *vaudun* (and all other cults derived from West Africa), "possession" is central, for unless the devotee or his intercessor among the *filhas* (handmaidens) of the *máe de santo* (high priestess) loses earthly identity during the ceremony and becomes the deity invoked, no communication with the higher world is possible, and none of the worshipper's problems will be solved.

Partly because Bahian (and African tribal) society is matriarchal, and partly because males have less time to concentrate and are more accessible to influences outside the African-Brazilian community, the officials of the cult are almost invariably female, and very few males are susceptible to possession. The *máe de santo* may be a *feiticero* (dealer in black magic), but in most *terreiros* (temples) putting a harmful spells on one's enemies is not countenanced. Sacrificing doves and goats at appropriate rites, leading prayers and dances, are among her functions. The *máe* is always a specialist in the use of herbs to cure minor ailments, and she is adept at foretelling a believer's future by "reading the shells" (*búzios*). She and her *filhas* regularly attend Mass, and sometimes all of the *candomblé* personnel participate in Catholic church functions—much to the delight of the Bahian Roman hierarchy, which exercises great tact, believing that their faith will win the ultimate allegiance.

One day in Salvador we were lucky enough to attend two *candomblé* rites. The first, very informal, was a baptismal get-together at the waterfalls outside the city known as Cachoeira de São Bartolomeo. Hundreds of Bahians of both sexes and all ages crowded around the steep cascade, whose rock face was decorated with votive candles and little piles of farina-like cotton balls. A battery of three drums, interspersed with chants in the Yoruba tongue, summoned the *orixás.* Many of those who let the falling waters hit them were instantly possessed, shaking spasmodically. We noticed one dressed in the uniform of an Esso gas station attendant. Children, unconcerned, splashed joyously in the lower pools. Market women sold food and soft drinks. A homemade cross bore the three words: AMOR, DEUS, PAZ.

A more formal ceremony took place at night at the *terreiro* of *Axé Opô Afonjá,* a very large one open at the sides behind the spectator's benches. Pennants of red and white paper hung from the thatched roof over the earthen floor. On an elevated platform at the far end, the ample, impassive *máe* in her billowing white robes was enthroned amid her court, from time to time shaking her symbol of authority, the cone like silver bell. As we came in, the drumming had already started, and the dozen or more *filhas* in their hooped skirts and sequined blouses were dancing barefooted in an ellipse, gesturing with their hands.

First the *Exú* received his conciliatory chant, in which he was implored not to make his unwanted presence manifest. Next the *filhas* made bow-and-arrow gestures for *Oxossi,* the hunter. And then, as the drum rhythms shifted subtly, they began to abase themselves before the *máe,* from a prone position first kissing one foot and then the other. The rhythms shifted abruptly now to greet *Iansa,* goddess of storms and thunder. Many of the *filhas* went into trance, some making plaintive animal cries and rocking around the enclosure as if desperate to escape. *Oxumaré,* the serpent god was called. But the *filhas* were now drifting out to remain entranced until their re-entry as *santos. Omolú's* music was played. Cat-cries followed, and a spectator in one corner began to thrash about convulsively. Chants of "Agolana!" Intermission.

The *filhas,* now dressed for their new role as saints, began to come back, all but one representing females. That one, *Omolú,* was gorgeously arrayed in strands of raffia, which fell from her helmet of cowry shells to cover her face and body. Others wore heavy arm-bangles, face-screens of copper beads. Some brandished battle-axes, poniards, powder-horns, mirrors, bundles of sticks. One of the masked ones left the dance to kiss us on both cheeks—exactly as in Haitian *vaudun*! The ceremony would continue till dawn.

When we expressed disappointment that we had arrived too late to see the *estampa* (or *pontos riscardos*, drawn points) laid out on the earth floor in multicolored chalks to invoke the particular *guias* (*loas* in Haitian *vaudun*), we were told that in this ceremony these ancient geometric symbols had been conveyed to deities on the same wave-length by the drums. We missed the *vevers*.

---

Facing page:

**Filhas Dressed as Saints** *(Orixás)*
by Isabel dos Santos.
Collection, Julia Hillman

### UMBANDA

*Umbanda*—sometimes called *macumba*, though the latter is a generic term for all the cults, with pejorative undertones in some areas—is said to have originated underground in Rio de Jañeiro when Getúlio Vargas' Estado Novo of 1938 banned "politics" and thereby created a vacuum. It is the dominant cult now in São Paulo, as well as in Rio and other southern cities.

Friendly to spirits from many quarters, placing no premium on orthodoxy, and as popular with poor whites as with the dark-skinned, *umbanda* actively promotes miscegenation. "When a white Brazilian receives help from a black spirit," a black lawyer in São Paulo told me, "his whole view of black values changes for the better." As in the spiritism of the followers of Kardec, with which *umbanda* vies for popularity in the South, *umbandistas* emphasize reincarnation. Like the Protestant, whose sects are growing in Brazil at the expense of the Catholics, they stress good works and charity, rather than merely utilizing their spiritual contacts (as the adherents of *condomblé* tend to) for selfish therapy or personal well-being. But though its cosmology is confusingly heterodox and its theology rationalistic, *umbanda* does not neglect the African *orixás* (among other spirits) and their capacity for sorcery.

We had an interesting exchange with a prominent *pai de santo* of the cult in Botofogo (Rio) just before a ceremony for one of the *caboclo* (Amerindian) spirits was about to start. The priest's personality and *terreiro* were in complete contrast to *candomblé* with its concern for keeping "Africa" pure and its flock insulated against change. For one thing, the *pai* was male and white, and for another he was a practicing radiologist during the day and spoke good English. Taking us upstairs he opened a filing cabinet to show us his press clippings. On a big wall map, red pins marked all the *umbanda* temples in the city. "There are thousands all over Brazil," he told us, "making us the largest of the cults by far, and I'm not counting those who practice *quimbanda* (black magic) in the *favelas*. For those who merely make individual acts of obligation to the spirits, there is *macumba* in the streets or on the beaches." We asked him whether *Arigó*, the famous Kardecist faith-healer/surgeon of *Congonhas*, could be considered an *umbandista*. He answered obliquely: "No one needs to be operated on who comes here believing; everything is taken care of by the spirits."

In the *terreiro* proper there were many signboards. Men to the left of the aisle, ladies to the right. An arrow pointed to THE BAR. Charts listed the spirits and their nights: *Tupinamba, Jupirá, Mata Virgem, Caboclo, Fleixas de Cachoeira, Sulta de Orientes, Preto Velhas, Exú*—all except the last foreign to the *candomblé* pantheon, but no doubt as ancient and powerful. UMBANDA UNIDA E UMBANDA FORTE![2]

According to an article in *The New York Times,* there were twenty-four thousand registered *umbanda* centers in Rio de Jañeiro alone, even at a time when military government frowned on all such expressions of popular initiative. "We must not condemn the primitive religions," a Dominican friar who teaches at Rio's Catholic University wrote, "but take lessons from them, adapt our religious language, ceremonies and liturgies to the needs of the people." The Archbishop of São Paulo has advocated joining the cults "to bring them to Christ." At Porto Alegre in the far south of Brazil, the nine bishops of the Latin-American Episcopal Council approved a motion for introducing cult songs and cantations into their liturgy. Before long, no doubt, the cults will be discussing countermeasures to block subversion on the part of the Christian churches.

---

[2]*Umbanda* united and *umbanda* strong!

## BATUQUE

Least known yet most accessible of the cults is *batuque*, practiced mainly in Belém, the big city at the mouth of the Amazon in the north of Brazil. It is said to have originated early in this century in the backlands of Maranhão to the southeast where Brazilian Amerindians always outnumbered Africans. The spirits of this cult, called *encantados* (enchanted ones), come from many places, including Africa, but the *caboclo* (Amerindian) deities predominate.

*Batuque*, even more than the other cults, is a religion of the poor. Significantly it caught on after a crackdown on smuggling and the granting of free-port status to Manaus upriver, which caused widespread unemployment in Belém. The worshipper's objective is to seek out the medium while in trance and gain support for the solution of everyday economic and family problems. Ceremonies, unlike those of *candomblé*, are therefore open to the public—some *terreiros* going so far as to publicize themselves at a local hotels—and "shows" replete with emotion, hysteria and drama are unashamedly staged. "The descent of immortal spirits would lose poignancy if no ordinary mortal witnessed the event," a devotee told two sociologists.[3]

In place of the West African drums which supply the rhythms in *candomblé* and in *vaudun*, participants in *batuque* clap their hands. There are incense and gorgeous costumes (almost as gorgeous as in *candomblé* but without the masks), and everyone looks forward to the witching hour of midnight when the baneful spirits from *Guinea* (the *Exús*) "mount" the mediums, bark like dogs, and hold burning gunpowder in their hands. Every living human is regarded as a potential medium, but only a few have the gift, going into trance at the slightest provocation, sometimes even when walking in the street.

---

[3]Seth and Ruth Leacock, *Spirits of the Deep: Drums, Mediums and Trance in a Brazilian City,* (New York: Doubleday & Co., 1974), p. 95.

Class, not race, determines membership in a *terreiro,* of which there are several hundred in Belém. Since problems are solved by supernatural means, effortlessly—indeed by putting the will in suspension—the membership tends to be politically conservative. Not surprisingly, the *batuque* cultists supported the military governments from 1965 on, since under the generals, as one devotee put it, "the streets are kept clean and wages paid on time."

As in the other cults including *vaudun,* the Western "God" is acknowledged but considered much too remote to concern himself with petty problems. Unlike him, the *encantados,* like the *loas,* have good and bad qualities just like human beings. A worshipper is quoted as saying "Drinking and smoking are contrary to Jesus. I've drunk and smoked... The *encantados* also drink and smoke, and they have children. The Saints don't do anything contrary to God."[4] *Batuque* is, in fact, as the Leacocks point out, one of the few religions in which individuals are believed to deserve supernatural blessings for practicing hedonism; and by the same token cultists—who say that Hell is here in this world—could not care less about the Christian preoccupation with escaping eternal damnation.

No wonder official Catholicism is waging a losing war with the cults, which offer so much in entertainment and drama, as well as in direct communication with the supernatural! The drift of white intellectuals to *candomblé*—the late great poet Vinícius de Moraes, the novelist Jorge Amado, and the sculptor-painter Carybé had already become cultists when we were in Salvador—is significant. So was the world-wide interest in Arigó who was achieving his miraculous surgery and cures through strange prescriptions while in trance as the reincarnation of a long-dead European doctor.

A key to the vitality of the cults is supplied by an American sociologist who had this to say about the religions of West Africa: "Their faith is not removed from life, but very infor-

---

[4]Leacock, *op. cit.*, p. 54.

mal, simple to understand and ritualistic...Fate rules the universe, but a way out is provided by the divine trickster in whom good and bad are not separated. Only the missionaries consider *Legba* a devil."

A less optimistic view was that of an American novelist who spent the better part of a year trying unsuccessfully to "receive" the spirits of *candomblé* and *umbanda* in a remote Bahian village. Failing to overcome his Western qualms and rationalistic skepticism, novelist A.J. Langguth in the end allowed that one ought to "accept and enjoy the Brazilian effort to recast and gladden an unsatisfactory world, at least until science overtakes us all." But it was Jorge Amado who said to us, "We are condemned to civilization," and he and the other white Brazilian intellectuals who have since embraced the cults would probably reject Langguth's pessimism. To argue that only the simple-minded can fraternize with the ancient spirits is to imply that the spirits themselves are simpleminded.

## *SANTERÍA* AND *SHANGO*

In the Spanish islands the African cults of *Santería* and *Shango*—unlike Haitian *vaudun* with its roots in Dahomey and Arada—came from the rites of the Yoruba tribes of Nigeria and the Bantus of the Congo. Both French and Amerindian influences, so rich in magical lore of their own, are absent.

In Cuba the Yorubas became known as *lucumi*, a term derived from the natives of Aku, a region of modern Nigeria then populated by Yorubas. But the spirits of the Yorubans, like those of the Dahomeans in St. Domingue, fused with the Saints of the Roman Catholic faith even in Colonial times.

Saints (*Santería*) in Cuba and in the other Spanish possessions, became the generic term for all the transplanted African cults, once syncretized with the religious cult of Spain. "To the Catholic worshipper, the image of a Saint is the ideological representation of a spiritual entity who lived at one time

upon the earth as a human being. To the *santero*, or practitio-
ner of *Santería,* the Catholic image is the embodiment of a
Yoruba god."[5]

Since *Santería* developed no *vevers* or other iconography of
its own, the Catholic images have thus become the sole representation of the spirits. As in *vaudun*, ceremonies involve
drumming, dancing, and the offering of blood sacrifices, but
since possession is a rarity, the wisdom of the gods must be
imparted through divination. A casting of cowry shells, bits of
coconut or beadlike nuts is read by an oracle-priest, a
*babalawo*. Therefore the efficacy of future actions, as well as
the success of herbal cures, is completely dependent on the
wisdom and skill of the priest.

There are far fewer gods to be served than in the diverse
Haitian pantheon. All come from Nigeria and are "white" like
the *Rada* group, that is, they are benevolent, never violent
like Haiti's *Pétro* gods.

The seven major deities, known as *orisha*, are similar to
various *loa* but are not identical. *Ogun*, god of war and steel,
is the closest to a Haitian counterpart, but he competes with
another male of great power, *Shango*, who is rarely served in
Haiti. Like *Ogun*, *Shango* is associated with the color red,
with fire, and virility. The female goddess, *Oshun*, might be
compared with *Erzulie*, for she is imagined as a Venus figure
and is associated with marriage. But as her color is yellow,
she is also the source of gold, which in Haiti is the special
province of *Brigitte-la-croix*. The second female goddess,
*Yemaya*, could be a version of *La Siréne* for she is associated
with water, shells, and canoes, but she is also the symbol of
maternity and is often depicted carrying a child. *Eleggua*,
known in Haiti as *Papa Legba*, is the guardian of roads
(rather than crossroads) and of the cardinal points. Here too
he is the first god to be invoked for he must open the path to

---

[5]Migène Gonzalez-Wippler, *Santería: African Magic in Latin America,*
(New York: Doubleday, 1975), pp. 3-4.

the spirit world. But the crutch *Legba* carries is relegated to another god, *Babaly-Aye*, and an aspect of *Eleggua*, known as *Eshu*, is seen as Satan. *Obatala*, like *Damballah*, is the chief and most distant of the gods, associated with whiteness and purity. Incantations to all the gods must be given in the Yoruba language, similar to the *langage* used in *vaudun cérémonies*.

Just as black magic is separated from *vaudun* in Haiti, so in the Spanish islands it is separate from *Santería*. *Mayomberos*, like *bocors*, concoct evil spells or *Brujeria*, whose magic is believed to originate in the Bantu tribe of the Congo. Although there are many bizarre stories of witchcraft that "worked," and many long and involved catalogues of the ingredients needed to cast effective spells, many assert that the effectiveness of *brujeria* is solely in the faith placed in it by both the very poor and the very rich. While the *babalawo*, diviner and father confessor, is consulted by those in need of advice or of herbal remedies, the *mayombero* deals in evil spells and in love potions. Some of them, like the following, documented by Puerto Rican-born Migène Gonzalez-Wippler, require especially strong stomachs:

> A particularly shocking love spell is reputed to be quite infallible and is highly recommended by some *santeros*. The only ingredients required are a few grains of hard, dry corn. The person casting the spell must swallow the corn and then wait patiently until the body disposes of the grains naturally. The corn is then removed from the feces and washed, toasted, and ground into powder. This powder is then given to the unsuspecting victim in coffee, wine or tea. It is said that the person who drinks this philter will always remain in the power of the one who gave him the potion.[6]

Much more complicated talismans called *gurunfinda* are prepared by black witches to protect their owners from all harm. One such

---

[6]*Ibid.*, pp. 47-48.

...is prepared inside a *güiro*, an inedible, hard-ring fruit of the tropics that resembles a *gourde*. Inside the hollowed *güiro* are placed the legs, the hearts, and the heads of a turtle and of various species of tropical parrots, the tongue and the eyes of a rooster, seven human teeth, a human jawbone, some of the cadaver's hair, and the name of the dead person written on a piece of paper. Seven live ants are also placed into the *gourde* together with seven coins, which are the payment to the dead for his services. The *gourde* is then generously asperged with rum and buried during twenty-one days beneath a *ceiba* tree. At the end of this time it is disinterred, marked with a cross of chalk, and hung from a branch of a tree near the *mayombero's* house. The *gurunfinda* is supposed to speak to its owner and direct him in all his magical work.[7]

What makes *Santería* "such a profitable business is the undeniable and peculiar power of the *santero*. Whether or not he is honest, most of the time his spells do seem to work." In Puerto Rico, Gonzalez-Wippler continues, "the *santeros* do very steady business with people in the theatrical and business worlds." Actors and actresses, gamblers, businessmen in dire financial stress, young women in search of husbands, wives with philandering husbands, all contribute to making successful *santeros* very rich.

They own real estate, profitable businesses, and have staggering bank accounts. A well-known and very expensive *ebbó* to insure luck and money uses the goddess *Oshún* and costs one thousand five hundred and forty dollars. By means of this spell, the *santero* transfers *Oshún's* power over money to the client. It is considered an investment, the same as buying shares in the stock market.[8]

But although the diligent author goes on to cite C.G. Jung to prove that the strange powers of the *santero* lie deeply

---

[7]*Ibid.*, p. 91.
[8]*Ibid.*, p. 144.

imbedded in the "collective unconscious," her insistence that the *santero* "can rightfully claim his share of the cosmic inheritance" and "control" the laws of nature, is highly unconvincing. "By the time slavery was abolished in 1873," she reminds us referring to Puerto Rico, "the Negro race was completely adapted to the customs of their Spanish and Indian neighbors, and most of the tribal rites had been forgotten."[9]

## *VAUDUN* IN NEW YORK

Even when the transplanted Dahomeans migrate a second time west of Africa, they carry their African spirits with them almost intact. Far more than *santería* and *shango* in the Spanish-Dutch-English arc of the Caribbean, *vaudun*, even in the two most materialistic cities of the New World—New York and Miami—remains a religion. It is estimated that the combined Haitian population of New York and Miami is more than a million, many of these emigrant "boat people" or refugees without entry permits, are so conservative and tradition-oriented that their morality and ethical integrity resist the hedonistic mindlessness and even the drug addiction of urban America quite firmly. Some Haitian assets, such as the creativity of its artists, are untransplantable—no popular artist has ever migrated to the United States or France and produced a genuine work of art in exile; but the *vaudun* faith appears to flourish as easily in the ghettos of Miami and New York as in those of Port-au-Prince. More easily, in fact, because in the United States there are no military strong-men to recruit the *houngans* into their nefarious service by fear or force.

> Here, in the basement of a large white house in the Bronx, a Haitian family gathered for a Voudou initiation ceremony. I sit playing one of three drums, apprentice to a Haitian master drummer. White skirts swirl around brown legs. Candles flicker next to a glass of water on the floor. Two glittering sequined flags are passed with a long machete for all to kiss three times. Honor.

---

[9]*Ibid.*, p. 145.

Respect. Loyalty. The singing weaves around the drum rhythm: *"Corps marché, zo li marché, la vie nous nin main bon Dieu-- The body walks, the bones walk, our life is in God's hands."* Without warning, the master drummer breaks through the music with a series of precise and powerful blows to his drum. He somehow plays against the rhythm, and everything seems to go into slow motion. Mambo Rosa, the Mother of the House, dances, caught in this net of time. She slows down. Her head shakes. Her foot is anchored to the floor and she cannot move it. She raises her head, and her eyes are huge, round, possessed. In a raspy voice she announces her name: Erzulie...[10]

The young author of this splendid account of *vaudun* in New York was introduced to Mama Rosa's *houmfor* by the lead drummer, Fritzner Augustin, after she heard his artistry playing for La Troupe Makandal and prevailed on him to give her lessons. She begins by making the same point about *vaudun*'s evil image in the popular mind as we made at the opening of this book. "Hollywood uses what it thinks is *Voudou*, writing evil characters into such movies as *Angel Heart* and *The Serpent and the Rainbow*, even into a *Miami Vice* television episode. She continues:

But *mambos* like Rosa maintain that real *Voudou* "is always used for good; so called bad *voodoo* is considered sorcery... Some people use the principles of *Voudou* to hurt people, but I am not allowed to do that." A woman in the author's office wearing a necklace of red beads, refused to be drawn out about it. Her reticence isn't unusual because most of what goes on in *Vaudou* is secret—not because it's dark and horrible but because secrecy is part of the tradition of initiation in Africa, part of a kind of teaching that slowly reveals levels of knowledge. Most Haitians, already battling the prejudices of racism, poverty and AIDS discrimination, are hesitant to allow outsiders (who so readily be-

---

[10]Elizabeth McAlister, "Voodoo: It's all around you, mysterious and powerful if you know where to look." *New York Woman*, March 1988. Ms. McAlister, a member of the staff of *Esquire* magazine, who had lived in Haiti, was initiated into the rite in the Bronx the year before she wrote this article, first of its kind.

ion...Its wisdom comes to people directly from the spirit gods, loas, who have as many personality quirks as the gods of the ancient Greeks.[11]

*Vaudun* thrives in New York, especially in Manhattan's Upper West Side and Brooklyn's Crown Heights. The *houngans* and *mambos*, there and in Queens, are often called upon to solve love problems, but just as often are called upon because of family disputes, depression, asthma, diabetes or even infertility. Mothers come to have their home blessed or to help get a child off drugs. A Catholic deacon in Queens born in Haiti admitted that "eighty percent of Haitians would answer that they are Catholics but less than ten percent go to church." Yet *vaudun*, he insisted, is primitive and unscientific: "I don't believe that there is a spirit behind every leaf in the forest." However a young Ph.D. in physical chemistry who was Mama Rosa's son and a *serviteur* saw no conflict between the cult and the sciences, recalling Einstein's deeply spiritual nature. "We know now," he told Elizabeth McAlister, "that science isn't the complete answer. It isn't going to solve all our problems. *Voudou* helps a person understand life from the heart. It helps people live out their deepest nature, and anyway," he added with a laugh, "there is a spirit behind every leaf in the forest."[12]

---

Facing page:

**Leaf *Loa***
by Prospère Pierrelouis.
Collection, Julia Hillman

---

[11]*Ibid.*
[12]*Ibid.*

# *Papa 'Zaca,* God of Agriculture

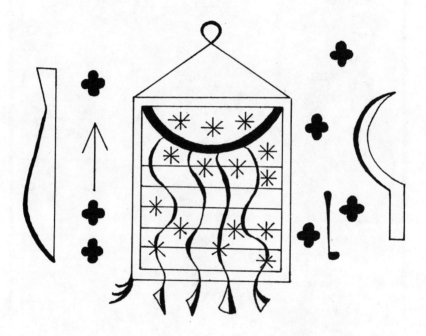

Since he is associated with the earth, *Papa 'Zaca* is related to the *Guédés* who inhabit the underworld and is therefore also a chthonic god. However, he is less sophisticated and is depicted as a country peasant dressed in denim and carrying a *macoute* (a straw bag). He is always hungry but will take his food into a corner to eat in secret. His color is blue, and he accepts corn meal and corn cakes as offerings.

# THE MAJOR GODS OF *VAUDUN*

*AGOUSSOU*          The Master of the Waters.

*AGOUÉ (AGWÉ)*      God of the Sea.

*AIDA-WEDO*         The Rainbow; Wife of *Damballah.*

*AÏZAN*             The First Priestess.

*BARON SAMEDI*      God of the Dead.

*BOSSU TROIS CORNES*   A Three-horned Cthonic *Pètro* God.

*BRIGITTE-LA-CROIX*    Goddess of Money.

*DAMBALLAH*         The Snake God.

*ERZULIE*           Goddess of Love.

*GUÉDÉS*            Spirits of Death.

*GRAND BOIS*        Spirit of the Woods.

*LA SIRÈNE*         Goddess of the Sea; a Mermaid.

*LEGBA*             God of the Crossroads.

*LOCO*              The First Priest.

*MARASSA*           The Sacred Twins.

*MYSTÈRES*          The Spirits, Gods, *Loas.*

*OGOUN*             God of War.

*SIMBI*             God of the Fresh Water.

*PAPA 'ZACA*        God of Agriculture.

# GLOSSARY OF TERMS

*Arbre-reposoirs*    Sacred trees in which individual *loa* live.

*Asson*    Sacred rattle, a beaded calabash, which is a *houngan's* or *mambo's* symbol of authority.

*Baka*    An evil spirit inhabiting the body of an animal.

*Baptême*    Baptism. All ceremonial objects are baptised.

*Barque d'Agoué*    A specially constructed raft to be filled with offerings to *Agoué* and then set upon the sea.

*Bassin*    A pool of water.

*Bocor*    A witch doctor who practices black magic (not a *vaudun* priest).

| | |
|---|---|
| *Bossale* | Untamed. A *hounsi bossale* is a priestess who has not completed her initiation. |
| *Brulé-zin* | A ceremony involving the boiling of sacred cooking pots. |
| *Bula* | The smallest of the three *Rada* drums; also known as the *petit.* |
| *Caille mystères* | The room of the *houmfor* in which the altar is housed. |
| *Calbasse* | A gourde. |
| *Canzo (Kanzo)* | Initiation by fire. Priestesses who have experienced it are known as *hounsi canzo.* |
| *Carrefour* | Crossroads. A sacred place. |
| *Cérémonie* | A *vaudun* ritual for the *loa.* |
| *Cheval* | Horse. A person possessed by a *loa* is known as a horse, because the *loa* "rides" the person. |
| *Clairin* | Raw rum. |
| *Connaissance* | Knowledge of rituals and herbal cures, some of it learned and some intuitive or supernaturally revealed. |
| *Coucher* | "To put to bed." Initiation requires that a person be enclosed in a holy room (*djevo*) for a week as a purification rite. Ritual items are treated similarly. |

*Créole*              The language of the Haitian people. Also
                      anything originating in Haiti—spirits,
                      people, food, etc.—in contrast to those
                      imported from Africa or Europe.

*Dahomey*             An African kingdom. It is retained as
                      part of the name of a *loa* who originated
                      there (i.e. *Erzulie Fréda Dahomey).*

*Diab*                Devil.

*Djèvo*               The sacred chamber where initiates are
                      "put to bed" (*coucher*) as part of a
                      purification rite.

*Dossu; dossa*        The child born after twins, who is
                      believed to have supernatural powers.

*Drapeaux*            Ceremonial flags used in ceremonies.

*Élite*               The wealthy mulatto class in Haiti.

*Esprits*             Spirits of the dead.

*Farine*              Flour. Used to draw *vevers* (symbols of
                      the *loa*) during ceremonies.

*Govi*                A jar which contains the spirits of a *loa*
                      or a dead person. It is kept on an altar.

*Grand Maître*        The highest god. The creator. Also
                      known as *Le bon Dieu.*

*Gros-bon-ange*       A person's soul.

*Guinée*          Africa. The land where the race and the
                  *loa* originated and to which they return.

*Horse*           A person possessed by a *loa*.

*Houmfor*         A *vaudun* temple. It may include all of
                  the environs, including the *péristyle,* or it
                  may refer only to the small room
                  containing the altar.

*Houngan*         A *vaudun* priest.

*Houngenikon*     The leader of the singing at a *vaudun*
                  *cérémonie.*

*Hounsi*          A *vaudun* priestess who has acquired
                  enough knoledge to participate in
                  *cérémonies.* She is under the *houngan* or
                  *mambo* in charge.

*Invisibles*      Invisible spirits.

*Kanzo*           See *Canzo.*

*La-Place*        The master of ceremonies at a *vaudun*
                  ritual, the chief assistant to the *houngan.*

*Langage*         Sacred language used in prayers to the
                  *loa*, unintelligible to man but understood
                  by the spirits.

*Laver Tête*      The "washing of the head" with special
                  herbs as a purification rite.

*Loa*             The *vaudun* spirits or gods; may indicate
                  one or many.

**Loup-garou**          A werewolf.

**Macoute**          A straw sack carried by country people; associated with *Azacca,* the god of agriculture.

**Maît-tête**          The primary *loa* a person serves; literally "the master of his head."

**Maman**          Mother. The largest of the three *Rada* drums; the larger of the two *Pètro* drums.

**Mambo**          A female priest; equal to a *houngan.*

**Mangé loa**          A ceremony to "feed" the *loa,* at which fruits, grains, and animal sacrifices may be offered.

**Marassas**          The sacred twins. All twins are believed to have supernatural powers.

**Marron**          A runaway slave who escaped into the hills at the time when Haiti was the French colony of St. Domingue.

**Monter**          A *loa* "mounts" a person when possession occurs.

**Morts**          The dead.

**Mystères**          The *loa.*

**Nanchon**          A nation or tribe.

**Nanm**          Soul. The essence of any living thing.

| | |
|---|---|
| *Ogan* | A piece of iron, beaten during a ceremony as an accompaniment to the drums. |
| *Ouanga* | A talisman. |
| *Papaloi* | A less common, more archaic term for a *houngan*. |
| *Paquets congo* | A small package which serves as a magical protection, often shaped like a bottle with arms. |
| *Passer poul* | A chicken about to be sacrificed is touched against the body of each worshipper so that everyone will partake in the benefits bestowed by the grateful *loa*. |
| *Pé* | An altar. |
| *Péristyle* | The public area where ceremonies take place. |
| *Petit* | The smallest of the three *Rada* drums; or the smaller of the two *Pètro* drums. |
| *Pètro* | The pantheon of *loa* who originated in Haiti and the rituals these gods prefer; more violent than the African *Rada* deities. |
| *Pot-de-tête* | A jar in which the soul of a person is put for safekeeping. *Hounsis* usually entrust their souls to jars placed on the altar of their *houmfors*. |

| | |
|---|---|
| *Poteau-mitan* | The center pole in the *péristyle*, through which *loa* descend during ceremonies. |
| *Rada* | A pantheon of *loa* who originated in Africa, named after the Dahomean town of Arada. |
| *Rara* | A festival following Carnival, held during Lent. |
| *Saints* | *Loa.* |
| *Seconde* | The second, or middle-sized, of the three *Rada* drums. |
| *Serviteur* | One who serves the *loa*. Devotees of the *vaudun* gods do not merely believe, but serve—participate in ceremonies, provide offerings, literally serve food to the *loa*, and obey the *loa's* commands. |
| *Servir a deux* | "To serve with both hands," both the *mains Pètro* and *Rada* gods; sometimes indicates one practices black magic as well as *vaudun*. |
| *Sobadja* | See *caille mystères*. |
| *Societé* | The communal organization which supports the *houmfor*; a *vaudun* parish. |
| *Tambour* | Drum. |
| *Télediol* | Créole phrase for passed along news; "the grapevine." |

*Ti-bon-ange* — A person's conscience.

*Tonton macoute* — Boogie man. Bad children are warned an "uncle from the country" will carry them off in his bag (*macoute*).

*Tonelle* — A primitive *péristyle*, sometimes merely an open-sided roof, held aloft by poles.

*Traitement* — An herbal cure, usually administered by *a houngan*.

*Vevers* — Symbolic designs drawn with flour on the ground during ceremonies to summon the *loa*.

*Vaudun* — The religion of the Haitian people, the worship of a pantheon of gods embodying metaphysical principles.

*Wedo* — The African city of Ouhdeh in Dahomey, retained as part of the name of *loa* who originated there (i.e. *Aida-Wedo*.)

*Ze-rouge* — A Créole phrase which means "with red eyes." An attribute of some *loa* in the *Pètro* pantheon.

*Zemi* — An object sacred to the Taino and Carib Amerindians, etymologically related to *zombie*, and to the *loa*, *Simbi* and *Baron Samedi*.

*Zins* — Ceremonial cooking pots.

SPIRITS OF THE NIGHT

*Zobop*   A member of a secret society of sorcerers associated with monstrous forms of the sorcerers dead. A ghoul.

*Zombi(e)*   A souless body forced to work as a slave. A dead body may have been stolen from a grave and reactivated by black magic, or a living person may be deprived of his soul.

---

Overleaf:

***Loa***
by Gérard, 1990.
Collection, Julia Hillman

# SELECTED BIBLIOGRAPHY

Abbott, Elizabeth. *Haiti: The Duvaliers and their Legacy.* New York: McGraw-Hill, 1988.

Bach, Marcus. *Strange Altars.* New York: Bobbs-Merrill, 1953.

Bastien, Rémy. *Vodun and Politics in Haiti.* Washington: 1966.

Courlander, Harold. *Haiti Singing.* Chapel Hill, N.C.: University of North Carolina Press, 1939.

Davis, Wade. *The Serpent and the Rainbow.* New York: Simon & Schuster, 1985.

Deren, Maya. *Divine Horsemen: The Living Gods of Haiti.* New York: Thames & Hudson, 1953.

Dorsainvil, J. C. *Psychologie Haïtienne, Vodou et Magie.* Port-au-Prince, Haiti, 1937.

Gonzalez-Wippler, Migène. *Santerìa: African Magic in Latin America.* New York: Julian Press, 1975.

Heinl, Robert Debs and Nancy. *Written in Blood.* Boston: Houghton Mifflin Co., 1978.

Herskovits, Melville J. *Life in a Haitian Valley.* New York: Doubleday & Co., rpt. 1971.

Leacock, Seth and Ruth. *Spirits of the Deep: Drums, Mediums and Trance in a Brazilian City.* New York: Doubleday & Co., 1974.

Leyburn, James G. *The Haitian People.* New Haven: Yale University Press, 1941.

Loederer, Richard A. *Vodoo Fire in Haiti.* New York, New York: Doubleday & Co., 1936.

Mabille, Pierre. "Pierres tonnerre, pierres à feu." (in *Les Afro-Américains, Mémoires de l'Institut français d'Afrique noire,* Dakar, n. 27, 1953, pp. 209-11).

Marcelin, Milo. *Mythologie Vodou (Rite Arada).* Port-au-Prince, Haiti, 1949.

McAlister, Elizabeth. "Voodoo: It's all around you, mysterious and powerful if you know where to look." (*New York Woman,* March 1988).

Métraux, Alfred. "The Concept of Soul in Haitian Vodu." (*Southwestern Journal of Anthropology.* Vol. 2, No. I, Spring 1946. University of New Mexico Press, Albuquerque, New Mexico).

Métraux, Alfred. *Voodoo.* trans. Hugo Charteris. New York: Oxford University Press, 1959.

Price-Mars, Jean. *Thus Spoke the Uncle.* trans. Magdaline W. Shannon. Washington: Three Continents Press, 1983.

Rigaud, Milo. *Secrets of Voodoo.* trans. Robert B. Cross. San Francisco: City Lights Books, 1969, rpt. 1985.

Rodman, Selden. *Artists in Tune with Their World.* New York: Simon and Schuster, 1982.

Rodman, Selden. *Haiti: The Black Republic.* Old Greenwich Conn.: Devin-Adair, 1954.

Rodman, Selden. *The Miracle of Haitian Art.* New York: Doubleday & Co., 1974.

Rodman, Selden. *Popular Artists of Brazil.* Old Greenwich, Conn.: Devin-Adair, 1977.

Rodman, Selden. *Where Art is Joy.* New York: Ruggles de Latour, 1988.

Saint-Mery, Moreau de. *A Civilization that Perished: the Last Years of White Colonial Rule in Haiti.* trans., abr., and edt. Ivor D. Spencer. Lanham, MD: University Press of America, 1985.

Seabrook, William. *Magic Island.* New York: Paragon House, 1929, rpt. 1989.

St. John, Sir Spenser. *Hayti or The Black Republic.* London: Smith, Elder, & Co., 1884.

Thompson, Robert Farris. *Flash of the Spirit: African and Afro-American Art and Philosophy.* New York: Random House, 1983.

Wilentz, Amy. *The Rainy Season.* New York: Simon & Schuster, 1989.